SHADOWCATCHERS

OTHER BOOKS BY STEVE WALL

———

Wisdom's Daughters

Wisdomkeepers (with Harvey Arden)

SHADOWCATCHERS

A Journey in Search of the Teachings of Native American Healers

STEVE WALL

HarperCollinsPublishers

HarperCollins books may be purchased for educational, business, or sales
promotional use. For information please write: Special Markets Department,
HarperCollins Publishers, Inc., 10 East 53rd Street, New York, NY 10022.

FIRST EDITION

Designed by Joel Avirom and Jason Snyder

Library of Congress Cataloging-in-Publication Data

Wall, Steve.
    Shadowcatchers : a journey in search of the teachings of Native American healers /
written and photographed by Steve Wall.
        p. cm.
    ISBN 0-06-016891-9
    1. Indians of North America—Religion and mythology. 2. Indians of North
America—Philosophy. 3. Healing—Religious aspects. I. Title. II. Title: Shadow
catchers.
E98.R3W36 1994
299'.7—dc20
                                                      93-48796

94 95 96 97 98 ❖/CW 10 9 8 7 6 5 4 3 2 1

To Lisa and Chris
For the beauty of their spirits
and the depths of their
enduring love

CONTENTS

ACKNOWLEDGMENTS

There is more to a book than just a manuscript. I am like everyone else. I am affected by the world around me and by those with whom I come into contact. Therefore, every experience over the course of my journeys helped to shape *Shadowcatchers,* and every individual who touched my life during my travels had a profound influence on its tone. Since I cannot recount all the experiences here, I would like at least to thank some of those who gave much of themselves in helping me proceed with my explorations—both inwardly into the depths of my own being and outwardly into the universe we all share.

Words fall far short in expressing my feelings of love and gratitude to B.J. So many things could be said, but I dare not go into them now. Besides having to deal with all of her own personal and professional commitments, she literally spent months helping in every phase of the editing process. I will leave it at *thank you* for what she has done to make this book possible.

Don Dahler, now a producer for CBS News's "48 Hours," was a godsend. He's the kind of person who, if you were drowning, would not throw you a lifeline: He would jump in to save you. By going with me to Central America, he did just that. Besides that, he also took on all of the pressures and responsibilities of driving the four-wheel-drive vehicles over some of the most treacherous roads I have ever been on.

Jose Carlos Morales, Program Coordinator for the Interamerican Institute for Human Rights in San Jose, Costa Rica, is just about the most selfless person I have ever met. He took time off from his work and personally saw to it that I was not only introduced to the elders in Costa Rica but had an escort to lead me to them. Most of the time it was he and his wonderful wife, Leila Garra, who were the guides. In no situation did they leave me unless they knew I was taken care of. I am deeply indebted to him, as well as to his entire family. My life has been enriched by having come to know them.

When it came time to process and print my photographs, I again turned to my artist friend Carl Bergman. There is no one else who could even come close to his abilities, and I just could not settle for less than the best. Although he was extremely busy with his own work, he agreed to process, print, and help edit my material. Now everyone can benefit from his contributions.

Through the years of working with Native Americans, there is one person who has been a friend from the beginning of my journeys. He is Dr. James Chastain. Sometimes I needed someone to lend an ear, other times I needed sound, solid advice. Dr. Chastain has always made himself available no matter the time of day or night. There have been situations where I discovered elders who needed his attention but had no money to pay. All it took was a phone call. Without a thought of the expense, he would take it on himself to fly to wherever they were and do what he could to help alleviate their pain. He never sought any credit for himself. I am especially grateful to him.

Along with Dr. Chastain, I give thanks to his wife, Emilee. Her spirituality glows, and because of that, along with the wisdom she has shared with me, she has affected my life.

One thing I've come to realize is that we're all fellow travelers, yet some have done more than others to take us into the unknown. My editor, Hugh van Dusen, is one of those rare souls. With little recognition and a lot of hard work, he has been responsible for introducing us, through his love for books, to worlds we would otherwise never have known. We are all better for his efforts. Also at HarperCollins are two other remarkable individuals. Stephanie Gunning and Wende Gozan are extraordinary in their professionalism, kindness and patience. I will forever be appreciative for the way they have touched my life.

I believe in angels. Most of us may never have the opportunity to actually come into contact with one. I have. Her name is Reba, and she works in a donut shop in Charlotte. During some of my hardest days of depression, I would go into the shop for just a cup of coffee. Her cheerfulness always touched me and gave me a much-needed lift. She never knew how hard I was having it psychologically or financially. I never told her. Yet, in her goodness, she would make sure she took the time to say kind things. I always left with my coffee and a donut. She made sure of it, because she paid for the donut herself. If you meet her, you too can say you've met an angel.

One thing I have learned from the elders is that everything lives because of everything else. I am no exception, neither is this book.

FOREWORD

I can give you my experience, and that's a story. I experienced it. You only heard it. But when you go and experience something, then you are telling a story. The difference is, if you're repeating a story, there's no spirit in it. When you experience it, there's spirit in it. So you put spirit in the story. This is your story.

> Leandis
> Northern Mexico, 1993

There's power in the wind. You can fight it and get nowhere, or you can flow with it and ride it into new adventures. In the beginning, writing this book was much like facing into the wind. Struggling to mold the material into what I thought it should be, I got nowhere. No matter how hard I tried to force it, it just would not go. Several times I considered giving up, but I fought on. I attempted in vain to fashion the material I had gathered into a form much like my book *Wisdom's Daughters,* and my previous work, *Wisdomkeepers,* coauthored with Harvey Arden. Still nothing worked, making it the hardest thing I had ever tried doing. Finally, I threw up my hands in desperation, thinking it just was not to be.

Then, it was as if the wind started blowing. I had no choice but to yield to its might. Feeling revitalized by the fresh breezes, I resumed my search—this time for the phantom shadowing me. Returning, I once again picked up my writing. Still, I never intended to write this book as it now appears. There is material here that I had determined, even before the possibility of my latest travels, no one would ever read. Much of it was just too personal and, in some cases, too painful to share. But, like my other journeys in search of the wisdom of Native American elders, the book began to take on a life of its own. The experiences I had gone through during those fifteen years, like pieces of a puzzle, cried out to come together in a natural unity with what I encountered in renewing my search, something that they have done in this work. I had to let it happen because I realized I had made many trips over the years but undertaken only *one* journey.

Having expanded my boundaries by venturing out of the country on my quest, I had to use translators with every elder presented in this book who lived outside the United States. Sometimes I had to have two with individual elders—one to interpret from the particular Indian language into Spanish and another from Spanish into English. In each and every case, I have tried to remain faithful to the meaning and intent of the original as it was spoken to me. Shirani Morales and Marcie Burgess worked overtime to give me translations as exact as they were capable of providing, and they were exceptional in their efforts. I owe both, along with many others, my sincere gratitude and heartfelt thanks.

When you finish your reading, you will definitely know a little more about me, and you will undoubtedly know the elders better. I also believe you may know more about yourself, because ultimately we're all connected.

Hopefully, you will see that this book was the product of the wind.

SHADOWCATCHERS

BOOK 1

THE HEALER

1

INVITATION TO A HEALING

The old healer was quick. Loping along behind him, I struggled to keep up as he raced down the barely visible trail toward the scrub forest. From his unwavering pace—his ragged boots kicking up plumes of dust as each step pounded over the parched ground—I reasoned, between pants, that he had no doubts about where he was going and what he had to do. Like one on a mission, he seemingly had only one thing on his mind and I was not part of it. Even when I arrived at his home in Northern Mexico, just after dawn, fatigued from a grueling twenty-seven-hour nonstop drive from North Carolina, he had seemed aloof. When I entered, he thrust a cup of his thick bitter coffee into my hands while pulling me in out of the morning's chill. Then immediately, to my surprise, he had waved me through his tiny house and right on out the back door.

"Come," was all he said, almost inaudibly, just above a whisper.

Dazed and in confusion, I hastily dropped the permanently yellow-stained porcelain cup onto an already cluttered kitchen table and yielded to his not-to-be-refused gentle command. Puzzled by the urgency of his overt preoccupation, I stumbled in weariness to take to my heels while attempting to pick black coffee grounds from between my teeth.

Finally, Leandis came to a stop on a knoll covered with thorny desert bushes, and I staggered up beside him. His dark, piercing eyes studied the horizon, missing nothing. Inwardly I questioned what the leathery *curandero,* a

3

Spanish word for curer, was pursuing. As I began to catch my second wind, my body stimulated now by the half cup of his soupy black mud reaching my bloodstream, I felt my anticipation of a warm reception and hopes of receiving personal help from the medicine man being dashed.

I had told him that I needed to see him, that I felt I had lost my way somewhere among the Indian elders I had met during more than a decade of crisscrossing the United States and traveling throughout the Americas. Maybe I had been expecting too much, but I never imagined I would be ignored. I felt that to the old man I didn't even exist. Somehow, from the three or four times I had visited him over the years, I had forgotten how distant he could be. Yet I still believed him to be the only one who could help me.

As we stood in silence, the intensifying heat from the rising sun began to sting the pale skin of my face. Leandis pulled his tattered cowboy hat down over his forehead to shade his eyes and continued to survey the landscape. I watched him carefully. Nothing much about him had changed since our first meeting during one of my magazine assignments in Northern Mexico fifteen years earlier. Leandis's craggy face had not one more wrinkle, probably because no more space had been available. His shoulders held the same stoop they always had. His baggy, washworn, threadbare jeans, covering his skinny, slightly bowed legs, appeared also to be unchanged. Only his waist had grown, the pounds a decade had added bulging over his belt.

Although I was apparently being disregarded, I felt a strange comfort just being in his presence. A tingling rushed my body, similar to an inexplicable "something" that had stirred deep within me on our first meeting. "I'm at the right place," I thought to myself as I impatiently awaited his next move.

Trying to break the impasse, I blurted out, "It's hard to believe—"

"That's why you're here," he immediately interrupted before I could go on with my thought, which I had intended to develop along other lines than what he injected! He said nothing more and the silence between us rose again.

I laughed to myself. He was absolutely right, it was hard for me to believe, but that was not what I had been thinking. It would have been useless to tell him that I was going to say it was hard for me to believe I was actually standing beside him. For weeks I had tried to find a way to reach him, since he had no phone and lived far from the nearest village, to ask permission to visit. Finally, having contacted an acquaintance from my earlier visits, I had been promised that Leandis would get the word that I needed his help. Weeks passed and nothing happened. Promises! I knew that no one would want to drive the distance to get to his isolated compound just to carry a message.

I had been on the edge of desperation, ready to make the trip with or without his invitation. Then one day, unexpectedly, I got a call. To my surprise, it was actually Leandis calling from Musquiz while on a supply run.

"You are welcome," he had said, "because there are some things," and the static on the line garbled his words, "but," and static again.

I strained to hear, the "but" lingering in my mind. Then the line cleared, allowing me to make out his words. "Say nothing to anyone—not about this. This is not about me. It is about something else, something higher. I'm not important."

Immediately I had thought he was going to tell me some deep dark very personal truth or some scary future prediction. Maybe, I reasoned in my ignorance, he was only a psychic. As he talked, I listened more intently and my anxiety was alleviated.

"If anyone comes here, that's okay, I'll tell them what I know. It's just that each has to find his own help. Everyone has a path. The search—that's part of the path.

"Understand," he had finished, "this is the time for everything to be revealed, but healing—it's not me. Nothing is mine. Everything belongs to the Creator."

I had been ecstatic. The trip was on. Within days I had hit the road, and now here I was.

With a jerk I came out of my recollections as I heard Leandis say, "We'd better go on. I've got a lot of work to do. You want to help? You up to it?"

Before I could ask why, I saw his eyes were already cast far beyond me to where the trees began to thicken just before the soft slope of the hills, not more than a quarter of a mile from us, turned steep. By the time I had found the object of his gaze, he was moving and moving fast. I had to run a few steps to again be by his side.

"Why? What work?" I mustered the courage to say, possibly overstepping my bounds. But I was upset. I was ready to talk about me. I had come a long way, and I wanted—I thought—I was expected. I was reeling. Taking in deep breaths, I added, after calming down a little, "Do you think you will have the time for us to talk?"

INVITATION TO
A HEALING

"Understand," he had finished, "this is the time for everything to be revealed, but healing—it's not me. Nothing is mine. Everything belongs to the Creator."

"That's two questions!"

Realizing I was on his time, I decided I would answer the question he had asked of me and let mine ride. "I'd like to help you, if you've got something for me to do."

"Tomorrow I have a ceremony. There's a woman. Getting sicker. Been to doctors—everything. Maybe it's the Evil Eye. She could have been cursed by a bruja, a witch, you know. Somebody paid for a curse. Maybe it was jealousy or envy. People do those things, don't know the bad will make a circle and come back. Doctors can't do anything with that. Don't know anything about it.

"This morning, before you came, I was out here praying for her. I got my instructions—'Make a staff and a wreath'—for the ceremony. We'd better get going!"

"Wait," I pulled on his shirt. "I don't know about that, but I've heard things. Somebody told me that happened to me. I've been in a depression. Wanted to kill myself. Could that have happened to me?"

"What do you think?" and he rolled his eyes as only he could do, making me smile a bit. He grinned, too.

Then he said, "You've got to believe. Nobody can do anything to you unless you believe."

"Believe!" I interrupted. "That's why I'm here. I want to know about God."

"Which one? Yours or mine?"

Surprised, I exclaimed, "There's only one, isn't there?"

"Oh, there are many gods, just one Creator."

"Then what has happened to me?"

Slowing his gait almost to that of a snail, he whispered, "I think you did it to yourself. There was nobody else. I think you separated yourself from your soul, lost touch with your God. What you were taught and what you've learned from all your travels was not the same thing. I've studied Christianity and other religions. Nobody can live up to most of those teachings. They doom you. Every Indian on the face of the earth has been touched by the church. Not much there about the Creator—just about the angry God. He judges everyone. That's why I came back to my people's original way.

"Anyway, you must have started questioning. Then, fear gripped you for using your power as a human being. Guilt ate you up for not living up to the teachings—thought God was going to punish you. Fear and guilt controlled you. Fear and guilt! What you think about the most is really what you worship. I can tell you fear and guilt are very demanding gods, so is greed. Now you've got shadows—like a curse—the Evil Eye."

Suddenly he stopped. Twisting his boots firmly into the dirt, like one taking a stand, he said, "You know about shadows! You take pictures with that little black box of yours. That's like catching shadows. That's what I do. I'm sort of a shadowcatcher, too. You do it with your camera, I catch them in my soul. I can see suffering, yours, in your eyes, and I see the shadows.

"You asked for yours, so you could learn I guess. Your profession was just the means for you to get where you needed to be. For me, what I do, I didn't look for. It was placed on me."

After a long pause, Leandis began walking again. As we occasionally rubbed shoulders while heading toward the hill, which was growing larger in front of us, he began talking again. "I knew I had it when I was six. I knew I could see things. We lived in a house that was divided so two families could live in it. A friend of my mother's became very sick. She lived on the other side.

"My momma took me with her when she went to visit to see how the friend was. I looked at her and I got very scared. I knew she was going to die, whatever that was. And she did, a few weeks later.

"Then, some months later, I went with my momma to a relative's. I saw the same thing. I knew when I looked in her eyes she was going to die. Before I didn't know what dying meant, I was only six, but I had learned when the friend died. Now I really was afraid.

"For a long time after that, I wouldn't look at my mother. I thought I was causing it. Everybody thought there was something wrong with me. They told my mother, 'What's wrong with little Leandis? He never looks at anybody. Something has happened to him.'

"It was about a year later when one day I accidentally looked at momma. I just started crying and ran and hid. The rest of the day I cried. I just knew my momma was going to die, because I really believed I caused people to die. But that day she didn't die. I was so relieved, but I was still in terror that the next time after that she would. She didn't. And she didn't die the next or the next.

"I was so happy. It was so good that I could look at my momma again. After I got older I realized that I could see things, but still I never told anybody. It was my secret. Even now, it's not something I would want. I would never ask for it. No one else should either."

With a weariness in his voice, he added, "Now I get people who are just about dead, about on their way back to the Creator. If they could come just a little sooner—" and his words dropped to a murmur. "Still, I do what I can. It's not me anyway. Everything's the Creator's."

Jumping a ditch, just before the tree line, Leandis shot into the woods. Momentarily I was left behind. Instead of analyzing every branch as a potential staff as he would do, I began searching for him. By the time I picked up his movement, he was gone again. I rushed to catch up. As I approached, I noticed his eyes were busy. For him every tree and every limb held the possibility of the ceremonial stave we were to make.

He glanced at me, knowingly, then said, "The spirits still walk these grounds," and nodded his head matter-of-factly up and down. "You can talk to them. I do. They are for our help, even yours too. They are just waiting for you to let them know it's okay for them to help you. See, they have to be asked. When you're ready, all you have to do is ask. You must be about ready to ask for help; that's why you're here.

"It's your time. You've seen a lot. Gone a lot of places. Now. You! It's time for you to understand. You've got to reconnect with your soul. Where you are, if you don't, it'll kill you. But, your problem's not physical, could become, it's your soul. The soul can effect the physical.

"You'll know more after the ceremony—the woman. The spirits'll be there. Some of them will be your helpers from the spirit world. There just for you. It's not just Indians who have the helpers. In your world, nobody talks about them. Just because you can't see them—can't see electricity either—but they exist and so does electricity."

"Oh, there are many gods, just one Creator."

I was mystified and slightly alarmed. I had no idea that I would be involved in the ceremony for the woman. Now I was to be part of it. And there were going to be visitors from the spirit world. The cagey curandero had sprung one on me.

Passing through a thicket, we were back out onto the path, at about the same spot where we had entered the trees. The old man raised his arm. I followed the direction of his extended, twisted index finger, which he had broken in the bridle of a horse he had tried, unsuccessfully, to break three or four years earlier.

"There. That's it. That is it! See? There!" he shouted joyfully.

Thrusting a knife into my hands, Leandis pointed again to the tree. Leaping back across the gully we had just crossed, I headed for the end of his pointing. Excitedly he changed his mind, "No. That's not it. Besides," and he waved his hand furiously to add, "see the young sapling. There. That's it. My mind was on the bigger trees. That's the way things work. Look for the one in your mind, and you'll find it. I had to be looking for one thing to find the right one."

I cut away at the tender tree, shaking my head at the reasoning. I knew from experiences with other elders that that is the way things work most of the time: It's absolutely one thing, until another better one appears. The better one was divinely appointed to materialize.

Soon the walk was over, we were back at the house. Fortunately, as the work on the branch began, we had shade to work under. First we trimmed away the tiny limbs. As we did, and to my surprise, a perfect curve for the hand appeared. Next we stripped off the bark.

"Go find a rock, about the size of the palm," the curandero requested. "It needs to fit the hand. You've got to smooth the places where the branches were."

For an hour I sweated the knots down. As one hand and arm tired, I would switch to the other. Finally, Leandis proclaimed it finished. "Now, we've got to cut rings to represent each one of us who'll be in the ceremony. We'll make our own symbols especially for this healing. When we get through charging this by planting it in the earth, submerging it in the water, heating it over the fire, and hanging it in the air, anyone who messes with this will know they got something. Wait until after the spirits use it, you'll be able to feel the power in this stick.

"Grab that shovel, I'll find a place near the garden so we can bury it. It's got to go in the ground next."

After leveling the dirt over the top of the stick, being careful it was lying north to south, the curandero suggested a smoke break. "Let's leave it for a while. Give it some time to nuzzle up to the earth. We'll come back for it later."

After some small talk, a few smokes, and a cup of his rich, strong coffee, he was ready to continue.

Gently, he pulled the staff out of the ground, cleaned the dirt off, took the limb in his hands, and headed for the water. I trailed along. By the time I reached him, he was already bent over the water and pushing the staff under. "That's east and this is west," he was saying. "I'm doing this for the four directions. You have to do it this way. Got to show respect. You do it for each of the directions. North, east, south, west."

I heard him begin his chants, but my mind was on the stick. It seemed that something was happening. I had no previous visions about what it would come to be, but I was beginning to see what was once a part of a little tree in a different way. A few minutes earlier it was alive, clinging to the side of a dusty ditch. Now, it was alive in a different way, but it was alive.

Slowly, his aged knees creaking, he got up off his hands and knees. Taking a minute to stretch, water dripping off his rough, experience-hardened hands and the gleaming cane, he was soon making a beeline for the back porch.

"Got to build a fire, it's got to go in the fire next," he was saying as he hunted around for sticks of wood. "You'll see some real changes when we put this to the fire. You can never predict just what, however."

Silently holding the stick, with his back to me, he turned and whispered, "The fire's ready. Let's do it."

Taking the staff at each end, his long arms stretched wide, he held it over the fire. Deliberately moving it over the flames, he delicately rotated it over and over again. Back and forth, from end to end, he carefully moved it so that no area received enough heat to scorch it or catch it on fire. Slowly the stick began to change colors. The raw, sap-wet beige turned to black. Where the rings were cut, its original coloration stayed the same, as did two of the knots where twigs had been cut off.

Satisfied that the purification with fire had been completed, the healer handed the now-black shaft to me and asked that I place it in a tree so that it would receive the blessing by air. As I followed his request, he eased into a nearby chair, "I think I'll sit, let nature work for a while. And you, looks like you could use a nap."

2

THE CURANDERO'S
DESERT WISDOM

By the time I awoke, my lack of rest having driven me into a long, deep sleep, the sun was clinging momentarily just above the horizon before nesting for the night. Dreamy cirrus clouds rode the darkening skies as flaming rich red-oranges reached up from the expansive high plateau. Trying to twist out the crick in my neck, which I had gotten from using a sack of grain as a pillow, I saw Leandis at work over an open fire. Pulling my aching body into alertness, I caught delicious aromas drifting on the wind from his direction. Groggily joining him, I realized he had been busy. Dinner was almost ready.

"Hunger'll always get you up," he said, laughing. "How about some beans? Want more, just say, 'mas frijoles,' there's enough."

As we ate, the sky went from dark blue to black and the range disappeared. All that remained was the two of us, the fire, and the stars overhead. Slithers of flame rose and fell. At times the old man was a flash of light, at others he seemed to be merely a shadow. I studied him carefully. A part of me was bewildered. Leandis was different from all the other Indian elders I had encountered in almost twenty years of traveling among them. Not one had been as cerebral. He could explain his philosophy in a manner I could understand. He had a way of transcending borders and cultures. I was sure he was letting me into a world few would ever share.

Saving us from the engulfing night, only glowing embers remained of the larger fire he had built earlier. Leandis threw on another stick of wood and said, "I like the night. The fire. The open air. This is a good place to talk."

I saw my opening. Finally, I thought, here's my chance. I would have his attention. As I stared at the flickering flames, I tried to mentally fashion what I

15

wanted to say. I was at a loss for words. Nothing would come. Then, I stuttered, "I—I need help. I don't know what to do. I'm lost. What I was taught in my youth doesn't work for me anymore. I was deeply involved in the church. I thought I was supposed to be a minister in order to find favor with God. Instead I went into journalism. Now, I'm caught between two worlds, Indian and non-Indian, and I don't seem to fit into either. So, I've been struggling to find the basis of my own spirituality. Besides, death, my death . . ." my voice trailed off. There were so many factors, I just didn't know how to put them altogether.

Slowly poking at the fire with a twig, not bothering to even look over at me, he said, "Healing, faith. You have come for a healing, but you are afraid you don't have the faith. You've lost faith. I'd bet you'd like to have the faith you had as a child. But you don't. Now you don't think you believe in anything. If you don't believe in anything, how can anything work? That's what you're thinking, huh!"

As I sat silently, mesmerized by the fire, the old man reached down and picked up a stone. Tossing it in his hand, he said, "You want to know about faith? I have a story for you.

"There was once an old teacher who was traveling with another teacher. They were like of two different religions or two different clans, but they were both supposedly wise men. They were traveling together, because they were going to a sort of a gathering of the clans—a spiritual thing.

"As they were passing by a village, the leader of the village came running out to meet them and questioned the one old teacher. He didn't pay much attention to the other one, just this particular one.

"He said, 'We have a problem here. I have people who are ill.' He said, 'I can't help them.'

"The old teacher said, 'Come with me.'

"They walked down to a little brook and he looked around. Finally the old teacher picked up a certain stone. He held it in his hand and he said, 'Pry my hand open.'

"The man tried and he couldn't. So the old teacher took it out, put it in his other hand and said, 'Now try to open it.' Again the man couldn't do it.

"Then the old teacher said, without giving him the stone, 'Now you keep me from prying your hand open.'

"The old teacher had no trouble opening the hand of the man. Then he gave him the stone. When the man held the stone, his hand could not be opened.

"'There's power in this stone,' the villager shouted.

"'Yes,' nodded the old teacher. 'Now after you use it, bury it in the ground, wash it in the water, heat it in the fire, let it dry in the air. It will get its power back.'

"He then gave him the stone. And the villager goes back to his village and he heals his people with it.

"So the two old men walk off. Finally the other says to the old teacher, 'You tricked him.'

"'What do you mean?'

"He says, 'There's no power in that stone.'

"'That's right. There's no power in the stone.'

"'Then you tricked him.'

"He stops and says, 'No. I agreed with him. I tricked you.'

"There's a lot of truth in those stories. And they'll leave you like that. There was no power in the stone any more than the stone had before. But there was tremendous power when the man focused on the stone. When we scatter things out, they run back and forth all over the place. When he focused on the stone in healing and he went to his village with that healing in mind, his focusing set the power in motion. That's what all these objects do.

"There's no power in an eagle feather until it's charged, until somebody focuses on it. The object is only there to bring a focus. It's like a magnifying glass. If you get it at the right place, you can start a fire with it. But if you move it too far either way, it doesn't work. It's a focusing. That's what objects are for. They don't have any power.

"Traditional medicine people, these people don't have any faith. They don't have faith in what they're doing. They don't have faith in objects. Have no need for that. Faith is something that bridges the unknown. They know faith is not necessary. They know, and there is a difference between knowing and wondering or having to focus on these things.

"You don't need objects to focus on if you know something. You don't need faith if you know something. You know things, because you've seen. You've got to build your courage to use what you know."

As the old healer and I sat listening to the fire pop and crack, he said, "I'd like to tell you some things I've been taught and some things I've learned over the years, some of the things I live by."

Then Leandis began to talk.

17

THE CURANDERO'S
DESERT WISDOM

"The one thing that the Creator cannot forgive us of is condemning ourselves, because he didn't condemn us. We condemned ourselves."

Letting Go of Material Things

This is a winding up. We've got the opportunity right here in this life not to have to do this again. If we don't mess it up! I'm talking about every one of us and our petty self-interests. Everybody wants to have a life that is free of pain and sorrow and have peace. You can't buy it, you can't sell it, and you can't get it through material things.

Between the time you leave the material ideas and get to a higher place in your thinking, you've got to labor and push and are always in the middle of everything. But once you cross the line of understanding, then everything is there. Everything comes to you. It's just provided for you. You don't have to earn by the sweat of your brow.

Our animal way of thinking has to be sacrificed somewhere. We have to give it up, because what it's giving us are only pleasures of this world. That means we don't spend all of our lives so that we can eat better food, get cars, move to big houses in the city. That's not what this is about!

When you finally give it up, it just comes to you. You can have these things provided for you. You don't own them, you never own them. They own you up to that level.

Punishment versus Opportunities

Listen. We're not being punished. We're being given opportunities. The bad things that happen to us in this life are not punishment. Punishment is the idea, "If it's painful, I'm bad and I'm being punished." This is not punishment.

The one thing that the Creator cannot forgive us of is condemning ourselves, because he didn't condemn us. We condemned ourselves. Condemnation is our idea. Until we stop condemnation of everything, of ourselves, and everybody else, then we're condemned already. The Creator doesn't condemn us for our own acts.

You can't condemn someone else, because if you do, you're condemning yourself. You're seeing that characteristic in them that's in you and condemning them for it. That's a mirrored self-condemnation. We're all connected. We're one with all things. The weaknesses we see in others are our own. That's a reflection.

We Are Earthkeepers

We go out and look at the moon or look at the tree and we say, "This animal is our brother," or "This water is our sister." When the missionary says, "The people are worshipping the sun," that's not what we're doing; we're worshipping the Creator. That sun is just a part of the Creator, and we're showing respect for it because the sun gives life. This should be understood. Somebody should understand that we're practicing Christian principles better than the guy that went in there as a missionary.

If we didn't do the ceremonies, it wouldn't mean the plants wouldn't bloom that year. It would mean we would stop having that respect and giving that praise. Then we stop having food to eat 'cause we would lose respect and cut down the rain forest, pollute the water, and destroy the balance. That is the real truth behind this message.

Life is a circle. Because we do these things, respect is kept alive in the mind of the people. That is what the ceremony is for, every year. This is what the white man never understood and still doesn't understand. And he's killing himself and destroying everybody because he still doesn't understand this thing . . . this cycle.

When we call ourselves Earthkeepers, we're talking about that way of thinking and it doesn't mean you have to be an Indian to think that way. But, it has to include us, because you can't exclude us. We are Earthkeepers.

A lot of people are becoming concerned about the earth. We've got a younger generation that intuitively knows they aren't going to have air to breathe, water to drink, food to eat if what is happening keeps going. When this thing reaches a point, it's not enough to stop polluting. It's not enough to say, "We'll stop this and nature will take care of it."

You have to change your spiritual views, change your ways. You don't just stop doing something, there must be a change in attitudes. You can't say, "I'm killing her. Mother Earth. So, I'll just stop killing her." Now you've got to doctor her. You've got to give her some first aid.

If you stop doing it, without a change in attitude, everyone will only stop doing it until it looks like it's recovering then start again. But when you get that reverence for it, know it is alive, that it's a living, breathing part of everything, that it's a part of you, the attitude changes.

The mineral, plant, and animal kingdoms were us at one time. That's part of our creative incubation. We're the third step of creation. Everything depends on the next higher step. We're responsible for everything up until now. What's being destroyed now is our own selves and everything else.

Finding the Truth

Once in a while you run across something and you just know that it is right. There isn't any question, you know that it's right.

I'm talking about the spiritual path. I'm talking about another level of thinking, of obtaining that thing we call truth. It seems difficult, but what's difficult is getting rid of the ideas that are in the way. The problem is what you've been taught, not what you haven't been taught.

The Creator in us says, "That's it." It sounds like a tiny bell within us, and it touches that part of the Creator within us. For a little bit the two of them ring together. It's like looking back at that and saying, "Well, that was simple. Why in the world didn't I know that!" And you think, "Well, I knew that. I just didn't know that I knew that."

Let's say someone reads one of our stories and says, "This is just more Indian talk, it's not about anything." In other words, these are just our old tales. But, if you take them apart, and you add what they really mean in your terms, then the truth can be found.

If something is true, it doesn't matter what language it's in. It doesn't matter where it came from, it's still true. And if something's false, it's the same way.

Dimensions of the Consciousness

In creation, first the rocks and plants expressed as far as they could. Then, locomotion came in. This was the power of movement. Instead of something staying in one place and having food, they could go and feed. Now we've got a little thing in the water. Then, it's on land.

Next comes the animal kingdom. That's the second step in creation. It doesn't matter how low the animal is, it expressed as far as it could express then rose higher. Everything benefited.

21

THE CURANDERO'S
DESERT WISDOM

When the animal kingdom expressed as far as it could at that stage, the third level entered. The human being was born. But something new was added—reason. When this human stage has expressed as high as it can, then it goes to something higher that means "All are gods in the becoming." That's the fourth step. It's the level of the gods. This is the place of the Creator. There's no instinct or emotion, just pure intuition.

We can't live off animals without the vegetables for them to feed off of. If you break that chain anywhere from the top to the bottom, the whole thing falls apart. That is the change that's going on. Human beings are destroying it, because they have forgotten the one thing that makes them human—the power of reason.

The first level could not stop being at the first level. It can't, because the second level is built on top of it. And the third is built on that, and the fourth is built above that. You can't take any of that out.

We can't live without what came before us. There is no way we can exist. If you destroy it, then everything dies. The whole thing dies. That's why people have to change their attitudes about Mother Earth. You cannot get rid of anything that the Creator created.

Laws of the Dimensions

We've got to understand the natural laws of every step of creation, the first, second, and third, and the principles that apply to the fourth. And when we start living those principles, we are connecting with that world.

Where you are now is as though you are in a glass box that's moving through something, something called life, beginning to end. It's glass on the top, it's glass on the bottom, it's glass on both sides, glass on the back, and the glass on the front is a mirror. This is the direction you're going in.

You can see out to your left, you can see out to your right, this is where you are now. You can look back and see where you've been. But when you look through the front all you see is a reflection of where you've been and everything is backwards. It's not real.

Clear up the mirror and you can see all around you. Then, everything looks like one. Right now, it doesn't. You've got a level that you cannot see. What you're seeing is what's back here, and it's backwards. So the only way you really see what's here is to turn around and go the wrong way.

If you're going to turn around and look, you're going to have problems. You've got to stay focused to the front, but all you can see is a mirror and you're trying to live by looking in this mirror at what's reversing in the past.

So, if you could just take the mirror out and put clear glass in the front, you'd be in another level. You'd see all four levels of understanding but what you're seeing in front is a reflection of the others.

There was this old man sitting under a tree. Another came up to him and said, "Tell us about this great, new place we've heard about, this new land where you don't have to sweat in your work, where everything comes easy."

He said, "Yes, I've heard of this. I've studied and I've taught a lot of people how to go there. You know it's strange. The people who have gone there and come back have told about it only in stories. They've said things that were actually real about it."

The other said, "Why didn't they just speak plain about it. Why do they tell all these stories?"

The old man reaches over and picks up a berry and he says, "I can try to explain to you how this tastes, but the only way you can understand what a berry tastes like is to taste it. Then, you'll always know what a berry tastes like. But, until you taste it, you'll never know what a berry tastes like."

You can't perceive a level you haven't been in. And you can't perceive what level people are operating in except by one thing—by their actions. Don't ever try to judge the spirituality of anybody or anything. That cannot be done.

The questions most of us ask in life—who am I, what am I doing here, and where am I going—do have answers. Somebody knows the answers to those questions. The answers are known, let's put it that way.

Laws of Consciousness

Spiritual teachers know. They understand what things are all about. They understand the oneness. They know this is a world of pairs of opposites, that there isn't any short or long, it just is. A thing is only short or long according to something else. Pairs of opposites. There's no good and bad, either, except to something else.

Human beings have to stay balanced in the middle. We can't go either way. Don't expect anything to be good or bad. Everything just is. That's the way creation works.

Right now, this is how "it" appears to you. So if you want it different, the only thing to do is see it different. You're playing a game. It's easier for you to see things as only good or bad, It's hard to reach up here for something you haven't experienced. That's why you keep going in the same old direction.

The teachers could heal by touch, because they knew that when the soul of the sick focused on what was wrong, they corrected it. They said the illness didn't exist in the soul, because the soul was the only thing that was real.

What happened was the ones who were sick believed it was magic and it worked, so then they could focus. They could know it was possible, not through themselves, but through the teacher. So now, the sick believed and, by believing, connected with the teacher.

Natural Law, Energy, and Consciousness

Some medicine people know that there are only three things existing in all of creation. First of all, there's Natural Law. Second, there is energy. And third, there is consciousness. That's all.

Healers know!

If I say, "You're healed," and because I absolutely know that you are, energy has to take the form of your focus and Natural Law provides it. Healers know this. They may not explain it like I do, but they know.

Most people can't understand this any more than that burro out there can understand how we reason. You look out here and say, "That poor old bird's going to die in the heat, there's a drought and no food, so I'm going to go and bring him in the house. So, I'll go out to catch him."

Well, he flies off. You say, "All I wanted to do was bring you into the shade."

That bird can't understand your reasoning. He's going by instinct. That's all he has. Human beings have those instincts, but we've got a little reason added to it now. But, we combine instinct and reason and make it into an emotion.

Instinct serves the animal well, but to us it can get in the way, especially if we only react to emotions.

The only thing that can interfere with intuition, the next step up, is reason. Reason was humanity's greatest blessing. But it's not a blessing when it takes over intuition.

Changing Concepts

This is not what you've been taught from birth. It's the opposite of what you've been taught. Teach a child something, right or wrong, and it is planted there like a seed and it stays and grows. So you went out into the world and saw things, learned things, and thought you were going to get rid of certain ideas. Well, you don't just get rid of an idea because of something new you learned. You ran up against a stone wall, because your teachings were started one layer on top of another.

You don't just go out and knock a bunch of rocks out of the middle of the wall. That's not the way it works. You take something out and you have to put something in its place. One way to do this is to listen.

When you're talking you can't listen. To listen you set everything aside, and when you get through then you can compare what you heard to what you know. But not while you're reading and not while you're listening and not while you're watching. Quiet down, that's when you can think. If you don't, you'll miss everything that was said to you because your mind was involved with what you thought you already knew.

Learn to listen. Hear with your heart.

The Subconscious

The conscious mind is not a thing in the world except a recording from birth. It has stored everything that's happened to you from the beginning up to now. It's in there. It operates this body. It knows how. It knows how to put every piece of it together, how to heal it, and whatever. All you have to do is give it the right order. Saying "Do it" is what medicine people do.

The reasoning mind, on the other hand, is the one that can go back and pick up past facts and can predict the future. You can run it backward and forward. That's what the animals can't do.

In other words, take your horse out here and tie him to that tree. A storm comes and just beats him almost to death. You go back down there and the old horse is just glad to see you. You untie him and he'll just nudge you, he's glad to get loose from there.

Take a person down there, tie him to that tree, he knows you did it to him. He's going to try to bust your butt when you come down to untie him. Different situation. He can reason. He can remember what you did to him. You shouldn't have tied him down there and left him in a storm. You'll have to pay the price now.

All life is one. Everything that's living is part of the oneness and given the same amount of life by the Creator. The difference is in how sincere the expression is, and humans have the ability of choice. We can drop certain things, we can change our mind, change forms of expression, but we can't get out of life. It's been here from the beginning and will be here forever. It's continuous. There's no getting out of it. Yet if human beings, who have the power to reason, change how any living thing expresses—like taking away the freedom of another human being or destroying the waters, the air, the animals, and the plants—everything becomes off-balance.

Right now problems are being created which no human will survive. The pattern is set. But humans will be back here! This thing will go on. This is not going to stop creation, because creation is not involved in time. It's us that's involved in time. It doesn't matter whether it will take a million years or ten billion years for balance to return. It doesn't make any difference. It's an eternal process. Life is here.

Now let's get something straight. The world that we created is coming to an end. But the earth itself is not coming to an end. What happens is we go from one level of understanding to another.

The thing about it is that when you die you carry only that level of understanding with you that you already had. You don't know any more dead than when you were alive. That's why you have to learn as much as you can on this side. You have to get beyond the shadows while you can or you will be stuck with them.

Kicking out the last of the fire, Leandis headed toward the house without saying another word. His familiarity with the way back was unmistakable. He needed no flashlight. I followed his shadowy outline as best I could, occasionally stumbling over a rock or a mislaid stick of firewood.

As he entered his small dwelling, I could only trail him by the sound of his heavy boots tromping across the floor. When he opened a hallway door, moonlight washed the little bedroom with enough light for me to see the narrow cot that would be my bed. It would be the next day before I would see Leandis's sparsely furnished quarters with all the makeshift bookcases and stacks of browning, brittle-paged books filling many of the dusty, rough handmade shelves. I would learn that the old healer had a thirst for knowledge far beyond the gifts he had been born with, and that I would be one of the few who would be allowed into his inner sanctum—much less be permitted to stay with him there.

27

THE CURANDERO'S
DESERT WISDOM

3

THE CLAW IN THE GUT

Near dusk a dirty pickup turned off the main road and headed down Leandis's rutty drive, raising a dust cloud high into the air behind it. Several people bounced to and fro until it came to a stop in his front yard. Leandis was prepared and waiting; I was apprehensive.

As she got out, the woman's pain was obvious. It showed in the tortured lines on her face. When she walked she yielded to it. Her body slumped, pulling her frame forward. Gravity unduly weighted her every step, as excruciating bolts of pain seemed to torment her with every movement. She suffered silently; the childlike sparkle in her eyes, still glimmering after forty-four years, only recently began to dim, betraying her secret. Only her family and the closest of friends knew the seriousness of her problem.

Having suddenly and mysteriously erupted a year and a half earlier, her affliction had finally become too much to bear. Though she still believed in the power of the curandero, she went to the clinic, as others around here were doing. Medical doctors had been consulted, tests had been done. Nothing showed up, the physicians had been baffled. Surgical specialists had been recommended.

She balked and told Leandis, "Sometimes doctors don't know what's wrong. They are guessing a lot of time. They cut you. I'm not going to be cut on just so they can see if anything is wrong. I know something is going on because I hurt. Sometimes it's so bad I can't sleep, then I can't even get out of the bed. If I'm up, it hurts. If I'm in the bed, it hurts. I've had enough, I can't take it any longer."

When all else had failed, she called in the medicine man, asking for help. The curandero agreed, recognizing that it could not wait. The time had come.

Leading them to the back of the house, the old man motioned everyone to find a place around the fire he had built for the occasion. "Bring the tobacco," he asked no one in particular. I took his command to be addressed to me, since I was the only one near enough to hear him.

Taking a ceramic bowl, he piled the tobacco into a little mound. I lit it for him. He took up the stick and held it in his upturned and outstretched palms, like he was making an offering to the gods. With great care he passed the staff over the now upwardly spiraling smoke, rotating it as he did. As he whispered his prayers, he turned the sacred treasure in the four directions. As embers flickered and gray vapors trailed skyward, he took an eagle feather and, with a gentle sweep, lightly stroked the staff. It was now charged.

After a long silence, Leandis instructed, "There are rules. Everyone here is a part of what is going to happened. Every instruction must be followed if what we do is to succeed. No matter what, tell no one about this. If you do, someone may try to undo it."

Slowly, and with great effort, the healer heaved himself up and made his way toward the narrow outside stairway leading down into a darkened masonry chamber under his house. Bracing himself, with his open palms sliding against the confining walls of the tight stairwell, he disappeared, floating into the blackness. Immediately the group followed and began forming a circle without being told. The glow of the flame from a lone candle flickered in the center of the room. Shadows jumped on the walls, casting a giant grotesque shadow behind each participant. The black, featureless phantoms seemed to dance to the shimmer of the tiny blaze as it pranced to even the softest murmur.

Taking a deep breath, the curandero closed his eyes and meditated, having encouraged us to do the same for a few minutes before beginning. Suddenly everything went silent. Outside, the chorus of night sounds had been deafeningly beautiful. Now, in the cavern, everything was quiet, the night sounds having died with our descent.

In an unusually soft voice, the curandero said, "I ask that the higher powers take charge. All unseen guests of the higher power are most welcome."

Turning his face skyward and with arms rising in harmony with his movement, he invited the guests of the spirit world to enter and join the circle.

SHADOWCATCHERS

Then he whispered, talking to all of us, "I am only a guide of direction. Whatever you see, whatever takes place, you're under protection. All that I promised is here already. Only those who are allowed from the other world can enter these premises. When we are finished the problems you developed through ignorance and misunderstanding will be removed. As to what form it takes and where it goes is its own choice, but it will not be here."

I listened intently as old Leandis began to tell first one, then another thing about each person that no one else could know. As he moved around the circle, I grew frightened. My turn was coming. Inside I begged to be spared. I didn't want anyone to know what he might reveal about me. I prayed harder as my time came. Then, he said, speaking directly to me, "There are no secrets. In time, everything will be known. Nothing can be hidden. Your life is written as you live it. You write it yourself, and it goes in front of you. Those who can see, know you . . . know who you are, what you have done. There's no right and wrong, just what you have done to create the situations you need. It's up to you to learn and change. If you don't change, you just keep having lessons."

I was amazed. He knew about my deepest fears and feelings, about the lessons I had brought on myself, and, with a twinkle in his eyes, he acknowledged he knew more but didn't speak about it. Deep within my hidden corners I knew, just knew, he had heard my plea.

After a lengthy talk with the afflicted woman, Leandis took the staff and waved it over the circle. The flame of the candle seemed to blaze higher, the movement of the cane inches above it. Now holding it upright, both hands clutching it, he moved to the cause of her physical problems.

"You are under a spell. Someone has put the Claw of the Owl in your gut. When these things are finished tonight, you'll be free of it. But, from now on you must always have proper protection. By the end of our ceremony, you will become familiar with the right way to do these things."

As the aging curandero talked, I realized I had a type of claw in my gut, as well, and this ritual was for me, too. He may have been working on the woman, but the healing was for me, too.

Giving her instructions for protection from further spells, he said, and I now listened more intently, "Others tend to take you away from what you know within your heart is correct and right and ideal. You don't need the opinions of others concerning your own spiritual idea. You need to look within and not from without. You may get information from outside, but seek the truth from within your own being, for only there is it to be found. And it is all there.

"If you wish further truth then look within yourself for it. Do not go to others. You may aid others that ask your opinion, but it is not proper to give your opinion where it is not requested."

In a very stern voice he said, "You have been cursed. A spirit is carrying it out."

I stared directly at the flame. Fearing what was about to happen, I wanted to leap up and run. But I was frozen. My body refused my commands. I slumped down and carefully inched closer to the one next to me. Everyone seemed to have the same idea. The circle tightened.

Leandis chanted, his voice growing louder and louder, summoning the higher powers for help. He commanded the spirit who was the carrier of the curse to come forward. He asked the spirit, "What is your name?"

There was silence.

After a long pause, he told us what he was hearing the spirit say.

"I am a powerful bruja," she replied.

"You are not," he flashed back.

"I am a powerful bruja. I work magic. Good magic."

In a soft, but stern voice, he said, "You do not understand. Magic is spiritual and is white. You carry darkness.

"What is your true name?" he asked.

"I will not tell!"

"And who are these two that accompany you?"

"My servants. They are spiritual helpers."

"These are only forms which have not been dissolved. They have neither life nor experience in the dark, merely forms which deliver the message."

A very cold breeze blew around my feet and crept up my legs. I was chilled, but there were no windows and no doors were open.

Leandis began to describe the invisible drama talking place in the now stuffy, almost claustrophobic room. The smell of dirt rose and burned my nostrils. The candle's flame twitched violently.

"She's threatening with her claw!" Leandis proclaimed. "The spirits are chuckling, now their laughter is roaring."

There was a long, very long pause.

"Study your shadows and study the stories the elders have told you. Remember they're more than stories. They have the meaning of life in them."

The healer reached behind his chair and presented the wreath of gnarled vines he had made while I had slept propped up on the sack of grain. Then, in a confronting manner, he held it out toward the evil spirit only he could see.

"Hard to take this with her claw . . . to catch it," he boomed, "but she does not want to take this with her claw. She keeps backing up."

There was another long pause. The air had become so thick, I was almost afraid to breathe.

In relief, Leandis whispered, "When the claw is melted completely, our helpers will take her out into the air.

"She's leaving," the curandero exclaimed in excitement, "and our guests are following her. The spirits told her that they are going to take her and try to help her find where she's supposed to be."

"Here, this is yours," Leandis told the woman and passed the wreath over to her. "She won't cause you any more pain, but first we must take away the pain you have now."

Leandis was exhausted, his whole body seemed to shrivel into a ball. His face had lost its color and his head dropped, nearly touching his knees. For a long time he didn't move, and his breathing was so slight he appeared lifeless. We all watched for any movement. Then, as if revived with new life, he rose and stretched. Opening his eyes, he looked right through and beyond us, seemingly seeing into another realm.

"There's more work to do," the curer broke the silence. "The curse has been taken away, but the shadow of it remains in the damage done to the organs of the body. By repairing the physical body, we will remove the shadows."

Turning and looking directly at me, he said, "You have shadows, but shadows are only the dark side of experiences to which you have attached emotions. Go back, take away the emotions, learn from the experiences, and pure reason returns. With perfect reason comes intuition. With perfect intuition

"Everything is a circle. You come, you go. I go, and I come back. And, one day we'll all end up at the same place."

comes a complete understanding and peace. Reach that level and whatever is thought must happen. That's the law."

Standing, the old curandero asked that everyone move and allow the woman to lie down in the center of the room. As she made herself as comfortable as possible, he lit more candles and circled her body with them. Clasping his hands, he invoked the spirit world. Again he seemed to become a different person. Without saying much, just a few words to allay any fears anyone in the group may have had, especially the afflicted, he bent over the woman and began the examination.

With eyes closed, he said, "We want to start with the head and go to the toe."

For the next hour or so, the curandero gestured and motioned over the woman. Pausing, holding his hand over an area where she was experiencing great pain, he said, "There has been damage to the liver and kidneys and to the nerves."

Simply using his hands over the right side of her body, he appeared in the dim light as nimble as a surgeon. His hands moved with deliberation from place to place. From where I was sitting, I could not make out all the intricate motions.

Then, quietly, he moved back to his chair. Leaning over, he pulled up his drum from one side and slowly began striking it. Quicker the beats became. Then, he started singing the ancient songs.

After several hours, he stopped. Rising, he straightened, holding his back, and stretched. His work was over. Then, in a weakened voice he said, "The work is finished and our helpers have gone, all except one. One of her spirit helpers will stay with her tonight in case she needs help. There's no reason anyone should be alarmed. She's still very weak. It's for her protection."

No one spoke. No one moved. Everyone was caught up in another world. After a long rest, the healer walked over to the woman, took her hand, and gently helped her to sit. Giving her time to adjust, he then pulled her into a standing position and slowly walked her to a cot where she would remain for the next day and a half. The session was over.

The night was just rising into the dawn when Leandis and I climbed out of the hole. Groggy from the loss of sleep, I went in to sit a while longer with the old man. Worn from his hours of work, Leandis turned wearily toward me and said, his head now resting on the back of the chair, "The staff goes to you. You'll be its keeper so you can remember not to be controlled by your shadows. They're yours, yours alone. You have to let go. They're going to go anyway. It's a matter of time. Up to you when.

"Go back to your home and get ready. Study your shadows and study the stories the elders have told you. Remember they're more than stories. They have the meaning of life in them. Look back over your experiences. Some of them, like everyone's, will be filled with darkness. Those are the ones you can learn more from. Study them. They are important. If it was not for the experiences, even the ones with shadows, you would not be where you are now. They will help you get to where you are supposed to be."

Even before he had finished, he was pushing himself up from his chair and slowly walking toward his tiny room. His long shadow trailed behind him as he made his way down the dim hallway. A single, bare low-watt bulb, like a solitary eye watching his every move, hung eerily from the ceiling. Reaching the threshold of his quarters, he paused for only a brief moment as if he would say more. He didn't. Then, with a gentle push, the door swung open. Without looking back, he was gone. The wooden portal creaked shut behind him.

Two days later, the woman and her relatives emerged from Leandis's healing sanctuary. Until that time, I had only seen one or the other emerge briefly for food and disappear again. Leandis was waiting for her. Without any help she climbed the stairs and walked up to him, reaching out to hold his hand. Her eyes were filled with tears, her mouth exploding into a huge grin. Quietly they talked between themselves. As if carrying out yet another ritual, she bowed her head, stepped backward two or three paces, and clung to his hands. Then she slowly let go and humbly turned toward the decaying truck.

Halfway to the pickup, she appeared to liven. She had no halting movements to suggest any remnants of pain remained. I could almost feel her desire to run, to proclaim her freedom. Opening the pickup door, she mounted the tattered seat. Within minutes she and her relatives were gone, and, in time, their dust settled.

Soon Leandis's place looked as if nothing out of the ordinary had happened. I knew better. I knew I would not be the same. There were things I had heard and seen. I now knew that healing, the way he had done it, was possible, although I wondered if I would ever understand how it was done.

I thought I was ready for what lay ahead of me. A dark cloud had been partially lifted and now I was thinking of taking that long hard look at where I was and where I had been. I was still a little unsure as to whether I could separate my emotions from the experiences and learn the lessons I needed to go on.

On the morning I was to leave, the skies had become completely overcast. Shades of gray hung over what was to me a bleak prairie. The desert had given up the heat it had absorbed from the unobstructed sun the day before, allowing the cool spring breeze to give me a quick chill almost equaling the old man's reaction to my departure. Saying good-bye was not a part of his vocabulary. I had learned that the hard way on a visit long ago. He had reprimanded me, "Good-bye! Never say good-bye. It's too final. And nothing is final. Everything is a circle. You come, you go. I go, and I come back. And, one day we'll all end up at the same place."

As I loaded the car with the meager belongings I had rushed down with, I figured I had already seen the last of the curandero for this trip. But when I started my old car, Leandis appeared in his doorway and slowly made his way to my window. Staying far away enough for me to see his full frame, he said, "We'll meet again soon. I want you to meet my teacher. I'll take you."

Immediately I wanted to get specifics, when, where, how. He just held his hand up in a halting wave that could have meant "Enough" or "So long."

"Soon," he said as he turned back toward the house. I was left alone not just to leave, but to leave with an anxiety of what was to come.

I didn't have to wait long to find out, although it had nothing to do with Leandis's promise to take me to his teacher. As I turned left out of his drive and

onto the main road to start my long trip home, flashes of my years of journeying among Native American elders began coming to mind. "Study your shadows," Leandis had said earlier. "They're important."

"Remember to remember," I told myself, as my mind shuttled between an excited anticipation of a future meeting with his old mentor and the still-fresh memories of past experiences. As I lapsed deeper into thought, I realized my path into Native America had actually started, oddly enough, right where I was—in Northern Mexico—with the Kickapoo.

BOOK 2

SHADOWS

4

MASANEA'S PROPHETIC WARNING

There was no road to Nacimiento de los Kickapoo. The village was not on the map either. It was far off the nearest blacktop—a thin line of a road, hardly a two lane, out of Musquiz—in Northern Mexico. Soon after the Kickapoo turnoff the pavement ended, changing to loose gravel, then to ground packed hard by rattly, rut-beaten pickups. Tire tracks crossed parched fields, and the only way to reach the Indian community was by bouncing over ridges, dodging holes, sliding across washouts, and fording streams.

Knowing that the Kickapoo had followed a visionary prophet, rumored to be Kennekuk, to Mexico in the early 1800s as a way of stubbornly maintaining and defending their traditions, which they have continued to do even into the present, I had submitted a proposal for an article on the Kickapoo to *National Geographic* magazine. It had been accepted, and I was assigned to do a preliminary photographic coverage.

I traveled to Eagle Pass, Texas, where I knew a small community of Kickapoo to be living. From there I had determined I would be able to learn the way to their village and quickly begin my story.

Suspicion greeted me when I started asking questions of those living near the International Bridge about their families in Mexico. "Go to Musquiz," was all that I was told. No one would say anything more.

As soon as I crossed the International Bridge, there was trouble with the Mexican customs: Where was I going? Why was I going? What was I going to be doing? Why did I have so much film, so many cameras? I did not have proper insurance on my vehicle. No, I could not cross; my papers were not in order.

Feeling hassled but staying determined, I politely turned around, crossed back into the United States, and made a mad dash for the border crossing at Del Rio. I had been meticulous in getting all the necessary paperwork done before my journey, so whatever the problem had been I guessed it was local and hoped I'd have better luck at Del Rio.

By the time I reached the little Mexican community of Ciudad Acuña, it was well after midnight. The only customs agent on duty was dozing. Startled that anyone would be crossing the border at that hour, he held me up until his superior could be awakened at home. I would have to wait. An hour passed, then two.

Finally, sleepy-eyed and obviously disturbed, a lean man in his fifties, still arranging his uniform, appeared. Now the two officials talked vigorously behind glass windows. Presently the authority confronted me. What was I doing starting a trip into his country at this hour, he questioned. More questions, all the while they were searching my car, removing everything and spreading it all out on the ground.

Satisfied that nothing was out of order, the superintendant sternly lectured me that I was doing a dangerous thing, that I should have started earlier.

Scratching his head, then rubbing his sleepy eyes, he boomed, "Why didn't you cross at Eagle Pass?"

Gathering my belongings, I pretended I did not hear. In what I thought would be a probably vain attempt to avoid his interrogation, I nervously stalled answering. Out of the corner of my eye I could see him with his hands on his hips, his chest proudly bulging. Minutes passed. I grew more alarmed, not knowing what to do except to keep myself busy loading the car.

Just as he stepped behind me, the phone rang from inside the four-by-four guardhouse. The assistant ran to catch it before the third ring. The superintendent watched with keen interest, straining his ears to overhear the muffled conversation.

I had been discovered, there was no doubt left in my mind, as I awaited the possibility of my arrest on some trumped-up charge for defying the commands given at the Eagle Pass crossing and embarrassing the guards there. Instead, the superintendent was summoned to the office. Soon he was exploding with laughter, causing nearby sleeping dogs to bolt awake and begin howling. Interrupting his conversation, the officer banged on the window and held up his hand. Immediately I pointed, telling the assistant that the superintendent was motioning me on.

The barrier was lifted and I was waved through. In my rearview mirror I watched the two, by then standing side by side, still puzzled, staring. Soon they faded from my sight into the eerie early morning darkness.

"Ask the Negroes, they live nearby. Herd their cattle. Cowboys for the Indians," and a hand gesture waving me toward the road out of town were the only directions to the Kickapoos I could get in Musquiz, a village due west of Salinas and around a hundred miles from the border town of Eagle Pass, Texas. Walking toward my car, I heard, "Go to Nacimiento de los Negroes, black village near the Kickapoo," wherever that was.

Standing by the door in contemplation of my next move and mustering the courage to make it, I glanced up, my eyes taking in the scenes unfolding around the town plaza. Kids were chasing each other, young lovers casually strolling arm in arm, the elderly sitting on park benches out of the heat of the blistering sun. My gaze settled, for no particular reason, on a tall, thin older man loading a pickup. He stopped, standing motionless, then turned slowly to meet my stare. When our eyes met, I was slightly embarrassed and quickly looked away. But no matter how hard I tried, my eyes would drift back. There was something about his mannerisms, the way he held himself, the color of his skin, his facial features. I felt we had met, but I knew that was impossible. Then I realized he reminded me of the Oklahoma Cherokee, of the Florida Seminole, and of . . . that was it! He could be Kickapoo.

I took the chance. I walked across the street. "Could you give me directions to Nacimiento de los Kickapoo?" I asked timidly. A grin spread instantly across his face as he pushed his dusty hat back on his head.

"What've you got to do with Indians?" he retorted, his smile sincere.

"Just want to meet some of the people, see if I can get permission to do a magazine article," I yielded, trying not to say too much.

"Well, you've already met one, me. I'm Kickapoo." Throwing his head back and cocking his hat even more, Masanea flashed his ever ready broad grin and laughed out loud. "I've got one more sack to throw on and you can follow me."

"I've got a question for you." And this time, I grinned back at him. "Do you think you could introduce me to some of the elders, even one of the elders? I'd like to ask permission to visit the people, talk to them about your culture, maybe photograph?"

The question seemed to tickle him. He roared. I stood dumbfounded, not knowing what I had done to provoke his outburst. Then, when he had calmed down, he said, "I'll ask around."

43

MASANEA'S
PROPHETIC WARNING

"The river knows the earth and
the river knows the river it joins.
There's no confusion, just a
knowing that the source of all
the rivers is the same."

"Do you think you could introduce me?"

"I think so. It'll be up to the ceremonial chief—he has certain duties, makes sure the ceremonies are held at the right time, since our hereditary chief lives with our relatives in Oklahoma—but I think you can visit. Just follow me out."

Musquiz was alive. The plaza was packed. It was Friday afternoon, the early beginning of an always festive weekend. People filled the streets. Boys and girls, in twos and threes, paraded the narrow sidewalks, bumping into each other and giggling and turning to get an extra glance to see if they had been noticed.

There were already traffic jams, bumper-to-bumper pickups. Police cruised in their aged but freshly washed 1949 and 1954 and 1957 Chevy patrol cars adorned with whip antennas and tassels.

Shopkeepers busily rummaged through outside tables loaded with sale items. Families, kids in tow and dressed in their best, took in the latest bargains.

Masanea motioned to me that he was ready, and then he was gone. He was not slow about it, either. I caught a glimpse of his truck going out of sight as I fought the rush and tried as best I could to maneuver the one-way streets. The only thing I could do was watch the top of his truck and try to catch up.

Once out of town the traffic cleared and the road was open. Still, I was a hill behind and he was rapidly gaining another on me. No matter how fast I went, I probaby would not catch him now.

He reached the turnoff well ahead of me. If I had not seen a cloud of dust to my left as I topped a ridge, I would have run out of pavement and been heading into the Mexican frontier, lost for weeks. His truck was loaded to resemble a C-47 cargo plane, with its nose high into the air and the tail on the ground.

Masanea was a wild man behind the wheel. I could only follow his billowing trail, all the while trying to manage the terrain of ditches, ruts, and streams on my own. When I passed through the black village, a community several kilometers before Nacimiento de los Kickapoo, I could only guess what the residents thought of the crazy North American racing by.

Fortunately Masanea's home was the first compound encountered after entering Nacimiento. Looking for his vehicle, I immediately noticed him. He was already unloading. When I turned into his drive, I slowed for the first time since leaving town. He just grinned when I pulled to a stop.

Masanea walked me through the hamlet and up a steep hill. His village spread out in front of us as we climbed. He took in the scene as if he were seeing it for the first time. He didn't just view it, he seemed to be inhaling it like taking a deep breath.

Below, thatched-roof domes seemed to grow right out of the ground, the earthy browns of the weathered tule matching the color of the soil. Around each structure, people moved about carrying out their chores. Kids ran about, chasing their dogs and each other. An elder worked on her knees by a channel dug from the river to redirect the water to run by her home so she, in her twilight years, would not have to walk so far. Her body was bowed as she bent low, washing reed for weaving into a mat for either a bed or a new roof. Nearby, a young woman toiled over a post that was sticking out of the ground; she pulled and stretched and twisted, tanning a deer's hide, her toddler floating sticks in the stream.

A few houses away, men punched holes in the ground with iron rods to form an oblong circle. Placing long tree limbs in each hole, they then bent the limbs at the top and tied them together at the loose ends—the structural formation of a new domed house—all under the watchful eyes and directions of the women.

A few yards away, a man directed the laying of concrete blocks, the early stages of yet another new house, breaking with tradition to build a square one with individual rooms, as others before him had begun to do.

Across the way, a family had just butchered a bear, and the mother was carefully cutting the sections of meat and washing them.

Pickups and a car or two passed in and out of the settlement, sending plumes of dust high into the sky and coloring the air a faint tan.

As we stood together at the crest of the mound, I again pushed the possibility of meeting with the ceremonial chief. Masanea laughed, as he had done in Musquiz. "You have permission to start," he said, "but it will be up to individual families. Whatever they say, goes."

"But I thought I should meet with the chief!"

"You have," he said.

"No, I've really only met you so far. I haven't talked with anyone else."

Then he let me in on his private joke. "I'm the ceremonial chief," he grinned, revealing his humor and letting me in on a facet of his personality.

Looking back over his village, Masanea sighed, his voice cracking as he began to talk about what was happening to his people.

Masanea Speaks

There's death here. Some elders about to go . . . just hanging on. When it comes, you cannot be here. No one from the outside. It will be closed. Only Kickapoo. The drums have started. Back in the woods.

Here! Listen! Hear them back in the woods! They're preparing the way, got the songs going. And, always, the drums. Got to have the drums for it to be right. Won't be long, sometimes the dying lingers, can't be pushed, hanging on for some reason. Lots of people have reasons, could be working things out, waiting for something, sometimes just being stubborn. Still, it's a reason.

The Warnings

What's your reason? Why you here? We don't need any story about us, couldn't get it right if you tried. Anyway we know about ourselves, nobody else could understand. We don't like to be amusement for others. Besides only when something's dying does it get talked about.

What's here for you? If you learn anything, once you learn it, what will you know? Your people are much further away from your place than mine. But we are on the way and getting there fast.

Still you can take a look around, but you won't be too welcome around here. Some people might talk with you. Nobody will hurt you, just maybe tell you to leave and help you do it. There's been too many try to come in for me not to tell you what to look out for.

Be careful what you get into. It's never what you think. So be careful. We're Indians, you're not. Ever thought about that? You want to know about something that you don't even know what you want to know. Wouldn't recognize it if you knew what it was.

It's hard for me to talk to you, hard to explain things. I've lived this way all my life, I'm part of this place. I know it. Not in my head, everything about me knows. Knowing it is like the river that comes out of the ground here and flows as the land slopes. Soon it will join another river and then another until it gets to the ocean. The river knows the earth and the river knows the river it joins. There's no confusion, just a knowing that the source of all the rivers is the same.

All people come from the same source, but somehow things got confused. Something got turned around. Maybe you lost your drum. Maybe that was it.

So now you want to know some things. Where do you start? That's a good question for you to answer. Maybe just listen. Listen to the drum. Listen to the air. Listen to the breathing . . . to the earth breathing. Listen to the stars go across the sky.

If you could hear the stars make their path across the sky, you wouldn't have to be here. You could be about the important things of your people. Yes, that would be a good place for you to be.

Hey, I don't mean you harm. Just warning. It is good you are here, but you are in for it. You're in for a long walk, maybe even a hard one. Yes, you're in for it. I can't help you, probably would if I could, but can't. You'll have to help yourself. Maybe someday you'll get to where you want to be, if you can figure out where you want to be.

Something in you brought you here. Call it whatever. But whatever it was, it's in you. It'd be real good for you to learn what it was. That'd help you more than anything. It's the same with everyone coming here and they all go away sad. You will too. Study yourself.

While I awaited word from the chief about the people's reaction to my request to do a story, I took a cheap room at the La Mina Motel in Musquiz. The time passed slowly. Then, early one morning a young Kickapoo messenger banged on my motel door, shaking the fragile structure. "You can't come today," he said in a hurry. "Someone will come for you when you can come back. There's been a death. You can't come." And he was gone.

So Masanea's warning that some elders were going to die had come true. If that happened, he had warned me, it would be eight days before any outsiders would be permitted in the village. Frustrated, I wondered if after that many days I would be remembered and if anyone would be sent to let me know I could return.

A long week passed and still I waited. Several times I called the magazine to keep my picture editor informed. He expressed impatience. I promised that everything was going well and that I would be able to cover the story with no problem.

At the end of a week, I called the magazine again and received a shock. My story was being transferred over to another picture editor, since my editor had gone

on personal leave. That was a bad sign. It would be hard to develop a rapport with someone else while out in the field. Maybe he would not even have an affinity for the story—lack of affinity has killed many a story before it even begins to develop.

The new picture editor wanted to see some results. I stalled, assuring him that a film shipment would be sent within days. He informed me that he had never had good luck with Indian stories. For him, he said, they were always difficult. His lack of interest was already showing, and he was pressuring.

I began to feel the squeeze, but there was nothing I could do. On top of that, no one would tell me what happened to my original picture editor. Working for the magazine created enough tension as it was. I felt like a rubber band beginning to be stretched.

I was still asleep when the phone rang by my bed in the motel. I struggled to come to life. It was another Kickapoo messenger. This time I believed that I was being summoned back to the village.

"Aquí, Esteban. Aquí en La Mina. La Mina Café. Aquí!"

"Juan? Juan! Es tu, Juan?" I stammered, attempting to speed the clearing of my clouded senses. Back and forth we tried to communicate between his broken English and my broken Spanish. Finally he made me realize that, no, I would not be allowed back. Another person had died and I would have to wait another week.

Then, excitedly, he said, as best I could make out without my interpreter who had the day off, "There is no time. My friend Jesus is with me. We must hurry," his voice too full of life so early in the morning, his words rapid fire one after the other. "Let's eat." Then, his palm slapping the phone like a clap of thunder, "Let's go. Hurry."

Alarm still drove me to dress at breakneck speed. I assumed that something else was wrong and I rushed to get to Juan as soon as I possibly could to get the news. When I arrived minutes later, having jerked on my clothes without a bath, my hair still tousled in every direction, Juan had ordered for everyone, including me. As I approached, he was already busily digging into his breakfast. Jesus, who had obviously been drinking way too much, only stared at his floating eggs. Juan jovially waved me on over, while Jesus remained oblivious to everything going on around him.

I sat down between them, mentally questioning what this was all about. Jesus's head nodded; he barely managed to say, "Eat. Eat. Huevos rancheros. Eat."

I couldn't eat.

"We were never meant to live in houses with walls and built in a square. We were to always remember the circle. Like life. Like the sun. The moon. The earth. Like our time on the earth."

Between bites, Juan told me about the death. I was deeply moved. Death always touched me, even if it was someone I had never met. Then, I realized there would be additional delays. My heart sank as Jesus slumped over. Juan ate on, cleaning his plate, and, with a wave, said, "Let's go," but not telling me where or why. I figured it best not to question, just follow.

We left Jesus with his face in his huevos rancheros at the La Mina Café. Juan laughed back at him, shrugged, and hurried for his truck. "Got to hurry. Got something to show you. You need some fun." Juan then took me on a wild Sunday morning ride to Boy's Town, the brothel district outside of Musquiz.

Boy's Town resembled a cross between an abandoned World War II army base and 1950s style one-story motel with row upon row of rooms and door after door. It was nearly deserted, a surrealistic barren landscape of dirt and stucco. A straggler here and there, leftovers from a typical cowboy-wild Saturday night, appeared from nowhere and disappeared just as quickly into the murky atmosphere.

Juan laughed, elbowed me, and pointed, "Alla!" His index finger slowly moved up to his eye, then curving outstretched toward a doorway where a young woman was just exiting, hesitating momentarily on the dusty concrete threshold. Unconcerned, she leaned up against the wall and hiked up her wrinkled, skin-tight miniskirt. She wore nothing underneath. Leaning against the wall, she slid into a squat.

Juan was excited. His "Alla" now more a shout, making sure I was observing. I glanced at his face, cheeks flushed, to see his eyes wide in wild excitement. When I looked back at the young woman, her water was already slowly cutting a path over the sloping, hardened ground. Sinking with relief, she jumped at Juan's "Alla."

Methodically rising and shaking herself, she began smoothing her rumpled skirt back into place and hurried toward the truck. Juan grinned. She stopped and stared, then yelled, "Norte Americano. Norte Americano!"

I felt my fear rising, not knowing what was going to happen next. I tried not to catch her eye, being the Norte Americano of her exclamation. She and Juan exchanged a few words. Both looked over at me. I suggested we leave. Juan just made himself more comfortable, settling in for more fun.

Attempting to get my attention, the young woman opened her blouse to expose herself as an enticement. In her mind there could only be one reason we were there. I tried not to look, not wanting to further encourage her. But just a peek. An elbow nudged me several times. Juan roared. "Sí?" he questioned me.

Smiling nervously, I politely shook my head, unwittingly spurning the woman's very serious offer. Rejected!

The words between the two grew intense. I suggested we leave. Juan laughed, and when he did, the woman opened the door and grabbed the rifle in the rack behind Juan's head. In a flash he reached for it. She was faster. He managed only to catch the end of the barrel. She clutched the stock, finger on the trigger. He tried to wrestle the weapon from her, the barrel flying back and forth from my chest to my face. I froze in the chaos, knowing that no one in the area ever carried an unloaded gun and thinking my life would come to an end right there in Boy's Town.

Just as the angry words grew into screams, the gun still being swung furiously, one of the gaunt stragglers, hearing the commotion, walked up behind the woman and whispered into the woman's ear. The movement of the gun came to a stop. Quickly I pushed the barrel away from my chin, trying not to arouse the woman's wrath again. Juan eased it out of her hands while her attention was focused on her new possibilities.

With my heart pounding, my whole body vibrating, I tried to catch my breath. Juan started the truck as the young woman and her new friend walked across the wind-blown courtyard toward one of the many stark doors.

For the next week, waiting in the sanctuary of my room for the additional cycles of death ceremonies to be completed at Nacimiento, I kept hearing over and over in my mind Juan exclaim, "Alla! Alla!" and seeing the end of the gun in and out of my face. As depression rose and fell from the delays of returning to the Indian community, I alternated between despair and hilarity. At least he had succeeded in his mission to entertain me, maybe risking my life at the same time.

Finally, after ten days of near desperation and thinking I had been forgotten, Masanea himself turned up at my door. "You can come now," he said. "The ceremonies are over. Now we are having the feast. You are invited."

My wait was over; I was being permitted not only to return but to participate in the feast of sending off the spirit.

The feast for the dead was just getting underway by the time I arrived. A plate was handed to me as I walked up.

As I ate, members of the mourning family began taking down the house where the person had lived so that if the spirit returned it would not be able to occupy the house; being unable to find the house, it would not bother the family.

"Don't see that little puppy anymore, the scrawny white one, do you?" a kid whispered to me.

I looked at him, puzzled. I didn't know if he was kidding or not. He said nothing, just raised his hand to my plate and pointed down into it and grinned. "Takes the spirit away," he added.

My chewing stopped. My jaws had frozen, my eyes glued to my nearly empty dish. I stood, transfixed, for what I thought was an eternity. Beads of sweat popped out on my forehead as a clammy coolness, even in the blistering heat, and circled my neck.

Startling me, an elder I had never met grunted, apparently noticing my ashen color, "You must eat everything. Can't leave anything. Must eat all the food."

Under what I perceived to be careful scrutiny, I cleaned my plate, never finding out for certain whether I had eaten dog or not.

After the meal was over, and his duties had been completed, Masanea motioned for me to walk with him. As we made our way through the settlement, he talked.

More Death Coming

There's more death coming.

See the houses that are being built? Those aren't the kind of houses for us. They're houses from the outside. God gave us the houses we are to live in. There are reasons. Now that is changing, but it is not from God. God didn't give us the new style houses. We were never meant to live in houses with walls and built in a square. We were to always remember the circle. Like life. Like the sun. The moon. The earth. Like our time on the earth.

Our real houses—and there's some that are left, they're not all gone yet—were always to face in the direction of the sun rising so that the light would be on our faces when we meet each new day. Only one door, it's on the east side and it's low. Have to bend down to enter, bowing to the sacred fire in the middle. Bend down to go out, bowing to each morning for a new day, for new life, so that we would remember, remember our creator and remember our way.

The Power of the Woman

The houses always belong to the woman, like the earth is our mother, the house is like the mother and the mother is always a woman. That's where life comes from. The mother gives us life and so the house is where the life is. Men don't own the house, women do. And I'm telling you, that woman can kick the man out. It is always with the woman's permission we men get to have a house. You're a visitor, I can't invite you in. You've got to get the woman's permission to come in.

We respect the woman. That woman takes care of the house, so we have a place to live. We do our part and she takes care of hers. There was a plan, it works pretty good when it's followed. That's the way it was to be from the beginning.

Get kicked out of the house and you see how hard it can be. Maybe some other woman will take pity and take you in. But it's back to the plan again. It's pretty easy to see. You can see it even better if that kind of thing happens to you. Once is enough. Don't want it to happen too often. Makes things tough on you. Word gets around real fast. Can foul you up in a hurry.

Could build your own house, but you got to have a place to build it. Women own the land, too. You got to get permission to build. See! Trouble.

The children belong to the woman, if you can say that children belong to anyone. Really just the Creator. But everything comes through the woman, even the clans. So woman is very important. Be nice to the women. But I know they need us once in a while, too. For food, building the houses, and if they want to have children. It all works out most of the time.

The Sacred Fire

Another of the things we were told was to keep the sacred fire going. It is never supposed to be let to go out. That fire is to burn in the middle of our houses all the time, year round. Nothing is to be put into it. No trash. No cigarettes. Paper. Nothing. Just wood. That fire was given to us by the Creator. Watch it carefully! It'll put you in a trance. Flames sometimes high, sometimes low, sometimes sparks. Something about it. It's alive. Has its own spirit. And that spirit is to help us. It's good for warmth, gives us life.

"Maybe God doesn't recognize us now. We don't wear the clothes he gave us. So how can he know us?"

The wood is alive, too, and gives its spirit for us. We depend on it. It's good, but we have to respect it. Take care of it. And never, but never let it go out. It's sacred. Let it go out and we have caused a lot of trouble to come our way. To keep it going was one of the things we were told. Bring trouble once and you think before you let it happen again.

When we go working the crops in the United States, somebody's got to stay here and keep the fire going year round, even during the summer, too. In the new houses, where's the fire. On cement floors? When the fire's gone, we'll be too.

Our Way Is Dying

Just look. Do we remember? Soon there will be nothing to remember, it won't just be forgotten. More than just lost. Our way will not even be known. Like it never was. Then, God won't even know us.

Maybe God doesn't recognize us now. We don't wear the clothes he gave us. So how can he know us? Will he know we're Indians? We must wear his clothes so that he will remember us. How can he guide us, if he doesn't recognize us? Will we still be his children? Parents are supposed to recognize their children. But, if they don't, how can they remember? What will there be to remember?

Breathe deep. That is life when you can feel how good it feels for the air to come inside your body. That is being alive. One day, there is that time, no more air, no more breath.

Our way is dying, just like the way our houses are going. Like our clothes.

The Prophets

We were led here. We had prophets. There have always been prophets, maybe just one at a time and maybe a long time between them. They seem to come, be sent just at the right time when the people are in trouble, when the times are the hardest or something really bad is coming. Watch for another prophet. It is time.

The prophet brought us here. He led us. It's been many generations now. Times were bad for the people. White people wanted our land up near the big lakes. Our ancestors were being pushed off the land, driven out, killed, forced to go to Oklahoma.

Some of our people went along with the changes, gave up the traditions, became more like white people, but the prophet—God led him so that he could bring the people. He saw it all, saw the future, saw the death of the Indian if they stayed. He saw the path to this exact spot, right here to this place.

In his dreams and when he closed his eyes, he saw the mountains, those two right there, with the river between them.

This is the birthplace of the river, comes right out of the ground. There's not another place around here like it. It's pure, it's special. All the other people around here want to be here. When there is no water anywhere else around, here the water keeps coming up out of the ground.

That was exactly what the leader was told in the visions . . . look for this place. It had been prepared for us and would keep giving us life. All he had to do was follow the directions from the message of the dreams. He knew it had to be so because of the dreams, and good for us he listened. Our ancestors followed him, and good for us they did.

The dreaming still goes on. We have people who dream and who know how to read the dreams. Watch out! The dream people will know you, see you, see all about you. It's in the dreams.

There will always be someone who gets the dreams, but many don't want to listen. Few follow the messages any more. So there are problems ahead, always are when no one listens. Maybe the dreams will stop, too.

I had finally been accepted, or at least tolerated, after all the waiting. Masanea and I were developing a trusting friendship, and I was building new relationships with others. I had actually lived for a week or more with one of the families. Here I was about to begin my coverage and the magazine was calling me home.

The magazine was concerned with the time I was taking to do the story. It had only been a research trip to start with, I was reminded. My original picture editor, the only person I felt could argue my case, had not returned, and I was being asked to return to present the material I had gathered so far.

My new picture editor was not pleased with the coverage. Frantically I pleaded for more time. I was warned that there would be no further extensions.

In my heart I knew that what I was getting was important. No one could shake me on that.

I had to tell Masanea. I had to tell him that I had been called home. Sadly, I looked him in the eye and said, "You finally let me in. Now I have to leave. I would like to stay, but I have no alternative. I hope you will understand."

The proud elder shook my hand and said, "Our way is not yours, keep that in mind. No matter how long you study us, you'll never know us. Your people don't understand that. They're looking for one thing, we're living something else. That's why we never liked to be studied. That's what most do who come around. Makes us feel kind of like animals being watched. Nothing likes to be trailed or hunted. We don't either."

Then, he placed his hand on my shoulder as he walked me toward the river. "The hunt is never for sport. It's serious, like a ceremony. It's a sacred thing. If you hunt for sport, next thing you know it turns into a war. I know you didn't come for sport or war. You seem to be really looking for understanding.

"It is easy to get off the way. It's hard to stay the right way. So many things to twist things around. People, I guess, bring it all on themselves. You're looking. That's good."

After we had stood on the banks of the stream for a while, he started walking me back toward my car. Along the way, he stopped. Then, he said, "Maybe your coming was only about our getting to meet each other."

The magazine killed the story. An editor wrote me, "I am confident we did the best thing to serve all our future interests."

"Do doable stories," an administrator with the magazine admonished me. "Do only doable stories. Your career here can only stand so many kills."

In my heart I knew that not only was the material valuable and the photographs acceptable, but that something more had happened. I was different. I was not the same after that. I had been told things that I had never heard before. I could never get the experience out of my mind, although I did my best to let go of my failure to get the story. I had started a journey without realizing it.

5

COMMITMENT TO
THE GRANDFATHERS

Leandis had started it. He suggested I remember. Now, over and over it played, hauntingly, returning like waves. I was back on the Grandfather Medicine Men story. It, too, had been for *National Geographic*. The assignment had started in early 1981, within a year of the cancellation of the Kickapoo story, when I met a Cherokee who had suggested I go to the elders of Native America. He had said that their ways were disappearing, that someone must go to them and record their words before it was too late.

"I've been waiting for you," the Cherokee said to me the very first time we met, making me suspicious from the start. It sounded like a con job come on. Then he added, "I'm glad you're finally here. Let's talk," further raising my already hoisted red flag. I would stay on the alert for weeks waiting for him to give me any clues as to what he wanted from me. As my trust in him grew, he felt comfortable enough to reveal his concern for the Indian medicine men, who he believed were dying out without leaving their wisdom safe in the hands and hearts of apprentices. He wanted someone to go and record their words so that they would not be lost.

Years later, I still vividly recall traveling to that corner of the country where North Carolina, Georgia, and South Carolina connect. I was working on the Chattooga River story. Not in my wildest dreams did I expect to meet the Cherokee, much less to become involved with him in any way.

Later, an Indian elder would tell me, "There are no coincidences. Only paths, paths of our own making. Really . . . only choices."

In the case with the Cherokee, I made a profound choice, a choice that would change my direction, a choice that would effect me personally and professionally for a long time, if not for the rest of my life.

Soon after the first meeting, the Cherokee sent me a message, an invitation. He asked me to join him and a few friends for a sweat, piquing my sense of adventure. Although I had reservations, I accepted. As soon as I did, a powerful anxiety swept over me, mixing with a rising fear of the unknown.

On the night of the ceremony, I reluctantly drove to the top of the mountain in North Carolina where he lived to join the Cherokee's gathering. As I sat in the darkness of the sweat's tarp-covered enclosure, steam began filling the lodge. In the pit in front of me, the red-hot rocks radiated a tungsten orange glow that highlighted the faces of those sitting cross-legged, shoulder to shoulder, around the tight circle. All eyes, frozen in expressions of expectation, stared as if in a hypnotic trance into the embers.

I took a deep breath, inhaling the cold mountain air. The peppermint cool entered my nostrils and flowed smoothly into my lungs. The scents of rising hot steam and damp earth mixed rapidly to create a natural high. I swirled lightheaded.

The Cherokee splashed more water onto the rocks. The steam exploded. My lungs rebelled from the intense, instantaneous heat. I choked, thinking I was suffocating. Gulping, I took in more of the vaporous fire. My eyes burned as the coals blurred into a fuzzy gaseous blackness.

"Just let it happen," I heard the Cherokee say, shattering the violent silence entrapping me. Momentarily, he restored my calm with a story of the meaning of the sweat, giving my racing heart a chance to calm. "There is no cause for fear. Or alarm. Let it happen. See what you see," he injected from time to time. After a long period of drumming, he added, "The spirits are coming in. They always join us in the ceremonies. Open your heart and your mind. Let them in."

An energy began to fill the enclave. I tried to look around. There was nothing to see. A swarthy pitch had risen, casting me into a strange illusory world frozen somewhere in time and space. I felt alone in the midst of the others, who I knew were still present.

I strained my eyes to see beyond a seemingly tangible wall of endless dark. If I reached out, I knew that I would touch it. I held back for fear I would cross over into an unfamiliar realm.

Slowly a murky image danced just beyond my comprehension. I closed my eyes, and the apparition continued to unfold. The Cherokee's words echoed, "Just let it happen. Just let it happen. Just let it happen."

"I'm making this up, I'm dreaming," I thought, and I wanted to get out. But I waited, waited. That's what I told myself I was doing, waiting. I couldn't move. Only my mind, which still seemed to be functioning, questioned, "How's he doing this?"

The dreamlike image played on. Whether it was my imagination or reality, it slowly became more visible. There seemed to be a crystal ball. I could make out the circle. As soon as that became apparent, a triangle formed within the circle of the crystal. I allowed my breathing to become more rhythmic as I settled into an uneasy calm. To my surprise, an eye filled the crystal. Cloudy at first, the eye became more clear as the haze faded.

Though dizzy, I was vaguely aware of more water being poured onto the rocks. As the Cherokee's drumming pounded louder and louder, the eye grew more intense. It looked right into me; its power was shocking. Gradually the eye began to evaporate into the darkness and a face took its place. As the face rose in prominence, I could see it was that of a very old person. It was ancient. The skin covering the fragile skull was as weathered as leather left to age on a fence post. Deep crevices sculpted the ancient visage. Yet, I was surprised to see that there was nothing to fear in the appearance. It seemed familial.

The face began to move rapidly toward me. As it passed, another took its place. Then it passed. Then another and another. There were old men, very ancient, some with flowing white hair, others with braids, some balding. Then, there were women, old and worn, but always with blazing eyes, eyes transfixed into my eyes. I thought I knew them. But, this was a dream, I told myself. Anything can happen in a dream.

Then, they were gone. In their place came the eye again, but only for a brief second. The dark returned and my smothering feeling resurfaced. The panic of claustrophobia gripped me. I had to get out of the lodge.

Halting my flight to freedom, I heard the Cherokee's voice across the pit from me. He was announcing that the sweat was over, and that we should be careful to exit the lodge the way we came in, by first circling the stones and then crawling out through the doorway.

When we again gathered around the blazing fire the firekeeper had maintained outside, no one said anything. The Cherokee tried to talk, but every one of us seemed content just to sit silently and warm away the quick chill of the night air off our wet bodies. Slowly the fire burned down and, one by one, the group began to disperse. As I was leaving, the Cherokee, sitting alone on a log and poking the last embers with a short stick, asked me to stay for a while longer.

"The Grandfathers are dying," he lamented. "Someone must go to them and record their words before it's too late." He hesitated, purposefully. Then, he added, "Why don't you go to the Grandfathers? Why don't you do a story?"

I didn't answer, waiting for him to go on. He stayed quiet, allowing the concept to develop in my mind. As it did, he added that it would be a monumental task, a grave responsibility to undertake and not an easy one to accomplish.

"Yes," I said, "I can try to do it. That would make a good story."

"You do not fully realize what you are saying," he cautioned. "Think about it seriously before you make the commitment. Once you accept it, you are committed. No turning back or it will bring harm to you in one way or another."

The Cherokee got up and paced for a few minutes and added, "If you say you will go, you will have ways out of the agreement.

"You will be given three chances to step out of the responsibility." He grinned, knowing something I didn't. "Tonight you will be faced with the decision three times. Each time you say yes, you will do it, you will be given another chance. Three times you say yes, then you must go to the Grandfathers. No other chances out."

He had to be crazy, I thought. Ways out, making commitments, responsibility—it didn't make any sense. Hell, all I was doing was looking at the possibility of a good story, but he seemed to be talking about something far more profound than I could imagine.

I drove off the Cherokee's cluttered farm, past the dilapidated barn, down the rocky, rutted drive and onto the gravel country road on my way to the blacktop leading down the mountain. A light snow was falling, the feathery powder beginning to cover the roads. Here and there ice from a previous storm still covered the curves shaded from the sun during the day.

At two in the morning, few cars were traveling the back two-lanes. I was all alone. Suddenly, as I questioned the Cherokee's judgment that what he was suggesting could be any more than just a story, I had no traction. My car was loose and sliding wildly.

A thought, suspiciously audible, raced through my mind. Do you want out? I imagined I heard.

"The Grandfathers are dying," he lamented. "Someone must go to them and record their words before it's too late."

As the question rolled in my mind, I saw that a sharp curve was coming up in front of me. I fought for control on the steep decline.

This is it, I reasoned. I cannot make that turn. There is no way but over the cliff.

"Do you accept or do you want out?" the Cherokee's conversation rushed back into my mind. "Do you?"

Quickly I said to myself, I would do it. I accept.

As if a miracle had taken place, the car straightened, the wheels catching the pavement, and I was in my own lane making the curve without a flaw.

Suddenly I felt weak, and my legs started jumping uncontrollably. My foot on the accelerator was leaping furiously, making the car lurch. Finally my nerves settled. It was over. I craved a cup of coffee, but, in the mountain communities through which I passed, everything was closed. The streets might as well have been rolled up. The towns were deserted, no one was stirring.

Picking up speed to get home quicker, I neared the river bridge on Highway 73. The thought flashed back, "Do you want out?"

Suddenly another car was headed for me on my side of the road. My mind turned in panic. My body stiffened. I thought that if I switched lanes, the other car might switch back. If I didn't switch, I might be hit head on.

"Do you want out?" the demand came.

My response rushed out from nowhere, "No, I don't. But I want to live."

When my front wheels hit the groove of the concrete of the bridge, the place where the bridge and the asphalt of the blacktop met, the other car was back on its own side of the road. It was as if there had not been a crisis.

Then, it hit me. I had answered the question, *the question,* twice. I slowed the car, knowing that I had to be very careful. There was one more chance, one more time for the question to be answered, if the Cherokee's pronouncements were right. Damn him, I thought, this was not the way it was supposed to be. I didn't believe in magic; I made decisions based on logic.

One more turn and I would be home. I sighed in relief, relaxing. It would not be more than five miles to the cabin.

Without warning, a cat jumped out in front of the car and the words leaped into my mind, "Do you want out? You have to answer quickly."

I was already swerving, and the other side of the road and a deep ditch were coming up.

"I want to live. Yes, I accept."

I regained control almost instantly, but the back tires had hit the cat. My heart ached, I felt regret. My emotions swept over me, nearly drowning me. I had always cursed people who hurt animals. I had, before that moment, always believed that killing animals with a car could be prevented. Now I knew better.

"Tonight was the time that cat chose to check out"—the thought came to me from another place, or maybe it was just my justification, but it continued. "It did that for whatever reasons, and you have had your chances, too. You chose to live and follow through with your path. The cat chose a way out. Don't blame yourself too harshly."

As I restlessly tried to settle into bed, very troubled, I wondered what kind of commitment I had made. Still, early the next morning I called Harvey Arden, a senior writer for *National Geographic*. He and I had become close friends while working together on the story "Troubled Odyssey of the Vietnamese Fishermen," published in September of 1981. I told him about the idea, and we proposed the article "Grandfather Medicine Men" for the magazine. Soon thereafter we were given the assignment and began a journey that had us criss-crossing the country many times. We met elders, recorded their words, and photographed them, their families, and their communities.

After months and months of gathering material, the magazine's editors decided that there was nothing they wanted to publish, that the photographs were unacceptable because there was no ceremony and no Indian regalia, that the information from the elders was of no value to the publication. The story was killed. Dead.

Feelings of rejection overwhelmed me as I recalled the death of the Kickapoo story and now this. Fortunately, the article on the Chattooga River, called "Wild Water, Proud People," was enthusiastically received and approved for publication.

Harvey and I refused to give up on Indian stories. We made another proposal for a coverage of the Iroquois Confederacy. We got the assignment, and soon our work began. Early on, my coverage began to run into trouble. My picture editor stated that the photographs were the worst that the magazine had ever received in its history. Still, the magazine's editor allowed me to go on with the story.

6

SPIRAL OF DEPRESSION

My depression, from a sense of personal failure, was growing deeper when Harvey and I boarded the flight in Washington, D.C., for Santa Barbara to photograph the historic Morgan papers as a part of the Iroquois article. On the way back we were to meet with Hopi elders in Arizona to discuss the Hopi-Navajo joint-use controversy, and finally on to Pine Ridge, South Dakota, for the 1986 Circle of Elders meeting. I was beginning to unravel.

By the time the plane touched down in Phoenix for the visit to the Hopi, I had made up my mind. I could not fly again. Ever. If I did, I just knew that it would be the last flight I would ever take. The thought of dying terrified me. My choices had caught up with me: I felt I had abandoned my religious teachings by even considering the spiritual concepts of the elders, and now I believed God no longer protected me. In my warped perspective, since I had forsaken God, He must have surely given the devil free reign to pursue me. The old phrase of the Baptists that "the devil is the prince and power of the air" stuck in my mind. In a distorted way, I equated "the air" with flying—since the air was his domain, that's where he would catch me. By not flying, I would be beating the devil out of his reward. By thinking I had reached the top of my profession by working for *National Geographic* and was failing at that elevated position I was at the end of the line. Fear ruled me.

"That's it," I blurted out to Harvey as we neared Flagstaff on our way back to Phoenix for our flight out. "I can't fly! I'll die if I get on that plane."

There was silence. For a long time. Then, I added, "I'll take you to the airport, but I'll have to drive."

More silence. For miles.

"Do you plan to go to Rapid City?" Harvey managed to get out.

"Yes, of course. It's important we be there," I answered. "I'll drive it, you can fly. No use my putting you through this."

"Do you know how far it is from here to Rapid City?" he shot back, then went silent.

I said nothing, unable to talk, my world going blacker.

"Then I'll drive with you, if that's what you have to do. We'll do it together." His genuine, heartfelt compassion consoled me.

Stopping at the next truck stop, grabbing cups of coffee, we turned around and headed back toward Tuba City for the run across northern Arizona to Four Corners. We determined to make it to Cortez, Colorado, for the night.

By the time Harvey and I reached Cortez, it was dark. Being creatures of habit, and knowing the motel limitations of the area from previous visits among the Ute, we checked into the Ramada. It was as if nothing had changed from years past. The rooms were the same—same curtains, same bedspreads—and it sounded like the same band still playing the same songs for the same cowboys. I was the one who was different. This time a dark cloud hung over me. My enthusiasm had waned, dampened by years of struggle and of standing between two worlds—Indian and white.

At breakfast, Harvey was unusually quiet. I knew why. We faced a long drive to Rapid City, and he was not looking forward to it.

About halfway to Durango, Harvey posed a question. "What is it about flying that scares you?" he quietly asked.

"I just can't get into one of those jets. I feel trapped, like being enclosed inside of a giant metal cigar and shot through the air with a rubber band. I can't get back into one of those things. I just can't do it!"

Harvey came back, "What if we charter a small plane? A prop? What would you say to that? Could you do that?"

I thought about the proposition for some time. As Durango came into sight, I said, "Maybe. Maybe I could do that. We could check it out. I'll let you know, if we can get a plane."

I was very uneasy as we turned down the road to the airport, resolving to do it one minute, panicking the next. As Harvey made the arrangements, I stood back, sweating in fear and not saying anything.

The deal had been struck. We had only an hour to wait while the pilot prepared the plane and filed the flight plan. Still I said nothing about the trip, choosing instead to talk about anything and everything else. Carrying on the meaningless conversation, my heart raced as I plotted and planned how at the last minute I would back out. I kept my strategy to myself.

The glass door to the waiting room adjacent to the private pilots' terminal of the Durango airport opened. An amiable guy, casually dressed, stuck his head in. Glancing around the room and seeing only the two of us, he said, "I guess you guys are my cargo. Ready any time." Then he checked the names just to make sure. "Going to Rapid City," he said, and absently injected, "with a stop in Cheyenne to refuel."

Harvey was out the door and trailing the pilot toward the airplane while I hesitated. I was thinking, "What the hell. I've got until the end of the taxi ramp to stop everything. I'll get out right there, if I have to," so I obediently followed.

I crawled in the back alone, Harvey and the pilot took the front seats. I knew why. No one wanted to sit by me with the gloom I had surrounding me. Even from the elders I had learned that negative energy attracts all sorts of things, maybe even disaster. Disaster, I repeated. I panicked, my emotions taking full control. I reached up and grabbed the front seat, pulling but not moving. My seat belt had me secure. My lips moved, but my voice was gone.

"Clear!" and the plane's propellers were turning, slowly at first then faster. We were rolling. The airport terminal was growing smaller behind us.

As I rehearsed putting my scheme into action, the pilot started talking. "It may be a little rough. Got some winds. Not going to be any problem. It's just the time of day."

I tried to listen, the roar of the engine nearly drowning out his words. By the time I made sense out of them, the nose of the single-engine, low-wing aircraft was high in the air. We had gotten clearance and were already lifting off. The wings tilted, the plane rocked back and forth slightly, the pilot throttled up.

"Listen up," the pilot said. "We're going over the Rockies. Got some clouds. We'll be out of radio contact with Denver some because of the mountains. Want you to help me."

I knew we were in trouble. Why else would a competent pilot need our help. Competent? I quizzed myself. What if he's not competent? And he needs help! Terror numbed my toes, then my feet. I could feel it rising.

"You got to watch out. Keep your spirit." Then he laughed, showing his gums. "Don't let somebody else get it."

"Sometimes the clouds will cover the peaks," the pilot was saying. "We're flying at about thirteen thousand feet. Don't want to hit any of those tips. If we go into a cloud, we will have to drop out of it.

"So if you guys watch the valleys, we can drop out of the clouds and into a valley. All you got to do is keep an eye out for me. That's all. Nothing to it."

The Rockies were magnificent. Photographs, paintings, words could not begin to reveal their majesty. Valleys, peaks, snow-capped mountains, one after another, on and on.

I leaned forward and asked, "But what about updrafts and downdrafts? What's the danger? What're the chances of survival?" I asked, dead serious.

Harvey swirled around, looked me dead in the eye, his words fierce, "Shut up! Shut up! You'll make something happen with that negativity of yours. So shut up." Then, with his face easing into a mellowness, a compassion showing through, he reached around the seat and patted my knee, "It'll be okay. You'll be fine."

As time passed, mountains still rolling by, I asked, my voice nearly screaming to be heard from the back seat, "I thought we were crossing the Rockies? Just crossing the Rockies!"

The pilot hollered back, "Yep, crossing the Rockies from the southern tip almost to the northern end. We'll be over them for most of the trip, all the way to Cheyenne. Out of Cheyenne it'll be just a short hop over to Rapid City."

The presidential suite at the Alex Johnson Hotel in Rapid City made no difference. Although it was elaborate, rivaling the Plaza in New York City for opulence, I couldn't see for the shadow of my depression. It followed me, cloaking me in a darkness I could not shake.

As I moved through the finely appointed apartment—two bedrooms, each with private bath, formal dining room, living room with an office wing, kitchen, an entertainment center with wide-screen TV, and phones everywhere—the shadow followed. The more I battled my inner conflict, the deeper my self-absorption grew.

Thinking I was dying, drowning in the blackness of a bottomless moat, I called home and talked for hours just to be able to breathe—the connection with my family rejuvenated my will.

Sleep was out of the question. By the time I turned off the lights in the wee hours of the morning, I had tossed and turned most of the night, afraid to close my eyes for fear that I would never open them again. Part of me wanted to die to save my family the agony I was putting them through, while another part of me was fearful that I would. I finally dozed off just before the alarm went off, signaling the time to head out to Pine Ridge for a meeting of the Elders' Circle.

Mathew King, one of the elders of the failed Grandfathers story, sat at a table in the kitchen, where volunteers busily prepared lunch. The elders of tribes from across the United States had come to discuss important spiritual matters affecting traditional people throughout Native America and the world. Of grave concern to them was the lack of respect nonindigenous peoples had for the earth—mother to all life on the planet. Harvey and I had been allowed to attend because of Iroquois Tadodaho Leon Shenandoah's presence at the gathering.

Mathew remembered me, although it had been years since my last visit. On this occasion I had brought copies of some of the photographs I had made of him wearing his headdress and wrapped in a deep blue woolen blanket. He smiled his toothless grin, his whole face glowing.

We sat looking at the photographs and each other. Nothing was said for a long time. For me, just being with him was enough.

"You don't look well," he turned serious.

Flicking the corner of the color photograph, he added, "You got to watch out. Keep your spirit." Then he laughed, showing his gums. "Don't let somebody else get it."

I told Harvey, "I'm driving back to Washington. You can fly, I'm driving. That's it. I can't fly."

"You can drive if you want," Harvey stated flatly. "I'm flying."

Heavy-hearted, I left him at the airport and headed east on I-90, not stopping to sleep until I picked up I-80 near Cleveland. Many hours later I arrived home, weary and exhausted. I went straight to bed. I was feeling alone in a no-man's-land, disgusted with myself, ashamed of my behavior, filled with guilt for my failure to be a tower of strength for my family, and horrified that my death was imminent.

Mathew King had been right, and I knew it. What he had really said was that I had lost my identity and had given the power over my life to someone else. I had been trapped in a net of my own making. Others had said that my photographs were unacceptable, that I was unworthy to continue my assignment, that the coverage was worthless. My transgression had been to believe them.

The pressure had finally taken its toll. What I was going out to get was never what the magazine wanted. Could I really blame them for holding on to the image of the world they had created and struggled to maintain? I wanted to run away to California, since it was about as far from the East as I could get and still be in the continental United States. And I instantaneously felt guilty for even thinking of abandoning my family, my commitments, my career.

I was sick. I knew I was. I began imagining I had a life-threatening disease and that the symptoms would show up any day. Every morning I would pull myself out of bed, hurry to the bathroom, and begin looking at my skin for any sign of a change from the day before. I would study my tongue at length, then examine my gums for changes in coloration from the day before. Next, I would hold my hands out in front of me, scrutinizing their texture. Finally, I would stare into the mirror, just looking into my own eyes, wondering what was behind them, seeking reassurance that my spirit still dwelled within.

At first the ritual was daily, then the ceremony was repeated two or three times a day. Ultimately it had to be done every time I passed a mirror, wherever I was. Eventually the compulsion drove me. No matter where I was or what I was doing, I had to drop everything and rush to a mirror or anything where I could see a reflection.

I saw my general practitioner. I was tested in the exotic disease center of a major research hospital, and, finally, in desperation, drove fifteen hundred miles to a natural healer. They all said the same thing: there was nothing physically wrong with me. Maybe some rest would do me good.

My eating became erratic. My weight dropped, and my appearance turned ashen.

No one, except my family and a few trusted friends, knew what was happening to me. Those who did know stood by supportively, vainly attempting to draw me out of the entangling web.

The darkness grew, the fog thickened.

7

THE STRUGGLE FOR SURVIVAL

Alone and dejected, but still trying to continue with my Iroquois assignment, I sat in my darkened motel room in Buffalo. The effects of my father's death just months before—after seventeen years as an invalid from progressively debilitating wounds sustained during World War II—still swirled in my mind. Seeing the space shuttle explode complicated my attempts to deal with death—my father's, then the astronauts', and ultimately my own.

In the middle of this process, I was still reeling from the culture shock brought on by working within the world of the American Indian. Mentally I was not prepared for what I learned of U.S. history from behind the "Buckskin Curtain," neither was it easy to accept the openness extended to me by Indians after the centuries of abuse and even genocide they had experienced at the hands of white men. Without my recognizing the signs, I had become caught up in their pain as well.

As the stereotypes of Indians ingrained in me by society, the educational system, movies, and the media began to die, I struggled to find a footing. When I turned to those with whom I was working at the magazine, those I trusted, I was rebuffed and felt them to be working against the very things they stood for—honesty, knowledge, truthfulness.

Of my peers, only Harvey remained steadfast in his support and unwavering in his friendship. He had been where I had, and we had shared the same experiences. Fortunately, he dealt with what we had found in a more rational way.

On the other hand, there was the predicament I faced with the Indians. Every time I made new friends, I also had to take on their enemies and deal with the sorcery, petty jealousies, and gossip.

75

Still, I knew I had to fight for what I thought was right, I had no other choice. Finally, I thought myself to be dying in bits and pieces with no place to run, no where to hide, no way out but death.

I struggled on, fighting back my black hole.

There was trouble upon my return to Washington. The picture editor and I had words. Everyone on the floor heard them and stopped what they were doing, waiting for the fight that would surely follow.

"Indians don't laugh," he said after viewing a photograph of Indian women I had wanted included, "and everyone knows it."

I shot back, "I see! You must be looking for Edward Curtis images of the stoic Indian. Well, if all you want are Indians in feathers and in ceremony, then you are a racist. If that is what this magazine wants, and that is *all* it wants, the magazine is racist. What's more, Indians do laugh and laugh a lot. They laugh more than any other people I have ever been around or worked with. Their laughter was real, is real, from the heart. I never laughed so much in my life."

I had sealed my doom, but I could not give up. I fought back the tears and walked out with my head held as high as I could manage, while everyone stood at their desks watching and listening.

I had a torturous drive home, knowing the consequences I was in for.

All weekend I stood in front of the bathroom mirror, looking for some mysterious disease I thought would show up at any moment. I checked moles for changes. I looked into my eyes for any cloudiness, stuck my tongue out to detect lumps and held it out so long my throat became sore. Then I believed the soreness to be due to approaching disease. My emotions, manifested as fear and looking for a physical outlet, had encased me in a prison of my own making. I was trapped and there was no escape.

Saturday passed, then Sunday, Monday. I was still alive when the phone rang on Tuesday afternoon, forcing me from my bed, where I had curled up in the comfort of the fetal position. The anonymous caller on the other end whispered, "Something is going to happen in the morning, it's already planned. You had better be here. It's very important. It's about your story. I can't say any more. Just be here. Be here early."

I roused myself as the line went dead. My depression momentarily lifted at the prospect of continuing with my story. All I could think of was the story. Spurred to action, I thought about calling Harvey, but I knew that could be a blow to his career if it was found out. Instead, I called Chief Leon Shenandoah, Tadodaho of the Iroquois Confederacy.

"I need to ask you a question, Leon," I said as calmly as I could. "When there's trouble, you know, if you have personal problems or there are troubles there at Onondaga, what do you do?"

He listened, not exhibiting any concern over the phone. I finished what I had to say. He said nothing for a long time. Then, in his quiet, ever-gentle way, he said, "We burn tobacco. Our way is not to ask that things be done a certain way. We burn tobacco and thank the Creator for the right thing to be worked out." He paused.

I held my breath, really wanting more from him.

Then, he asked, "You've got some problems?" Not waiting for an answer, he added, "I'll burn tobacco for you. You'll have help—help from the other world— for the right thing to work out. They'll go in front of you. Have no fear."

Admonishing me a little in a sharper tone, he injected, "You've got to develop a skin seven layers thick," and he hung up.

"Urgent," I furiously wrote at the top of the memo to the editor after learning that a meeting of top executives had been called by my picture editor to review my work. Trays of slides had been prepared, selections I had not approved, for the organized kill. I had even heard rumors that the picture editor had already started asking about photographers who might be available to complete my story.

"Urgent," centered on the white sheet of paper stared back at me, anger blurring my mind. Momentarily I was lost as to what to say next. Then I slowly started writing that I knew the executive council had been called into session for the sole purpose of reviewing my Iroquois photographs. I made it pointedly clear I had been specifically told by my picture editor that I was absolutely forbidden from attending the meeting. Stating emphatically that I disavowed "the erratic and, in my view, totally incompetent selection" which had been made without my participation or approval, I requested, in closing, the chance to defend my work and reputation and be permitted to submit my choice of photographs for his consideration.

The editor's reply was quick, but not without a troubling development. He wrote in longhand at the bottom of my memo, "As has been said on other subjects—this morning's situation got so messed up it was unfixable—like Humpty Dumpty. When I heard you were here I called off the event—in mid-event—I simply can't see you now but I 'always' insist that the photographer have a say in

77

THE STRUGGLE
FOR SURVIVAL

selects and be present at projection sessions for better or worse. By now you have heard my feelings from several directions—I do not feel Iroquois is in deep trouble—but more is needed."

Then the ax fell. "I heard second- or thirdhand that you feel we are a racist organization. I resent that deeply. If you really feel that way you don't need to compromise your standards by working for us any longer. I must be away for two days or I would take time to resolve some issues now. I hope that isn't necessary. Let's finish Iroquois and look at it."

An editing room was placed at my disposal, and my coverage, over five hundred yellow boxes of Kodachrome slides, began arriving from storage. A sign was placed on the door that read, "Reserved for Steve Wall."

On the very first day, after returning from lunch, I found someone had marked through my name and had written, "Injuns."

Later, while walking through the building I was greeted by a senior administrator with, "Well, if it isn't our Mr. Indian."

For four days I worked, editing my transparencies. Finally, I had a tray prepared and reviewed it, as amicably as possible, with my picture editor. He approved it, and a story session was scheduled with the magazine's editor. The article was accepted, but its publication, in September 1987, gave me only a small joy after so many losses and so much pain. What should have been a triumph was actually a shallow victory. After one more story for the magazine, I was out of work. Although I had a signed contract to cover the Cherokee, I was paid not to do it. There would be no more assignments from *National Geographic* magazine.

Over the years, oddly enough, I had never had any problems with my work being accepted and published by the Special Publications division of the National Geographic Society. When the Corcoran Gallery of Art organized the massive exhibit "Odyssey: The Art of Photography at the *National Geographic*," which opened in Washington, D.C., in 1988 and toured galleries around the world, one of my photographs was included. My downfall, in more ways than one, was Indian stories, because I had worked to reveal the intimate, even the spiritual, instead of adhering to an unwritten code of producing cool, detached coverage.

I wanted work, but none came. Debts mounted. Even in my despair, I had ideas and presented proposals to magazines and publications. Thirty-two of them, to be exact. Most publications didn't even respond; only three or four sent back rejections. Not one assignment materialized.

8

GIFT OF GOOD MEDICINE

Some months later, word reached me from several sources that I would never work for the magazine again. About the same time, my family and I lost our house, and our car was repossessed. Almost simultaneously, my daughter dropped out of college to return home and take a job to contribute whatever she could to the family income. My wife went to work in a fast-food chain's management program, which made it necessary for her to report to work before sunrise and drained her physically, without equal financial compensation. My high school–age son worked after school at an ice cream parlor. Nothing was enough to reverse the downward spiral.

My guilt, complicated with having to take charity and move my family in with a friend, escalated. I plunged deeper into despair. Thoughts of suicide surfaced. I held them at bay, but the ground for a way out remained fertile.

One day, as the move to put the furniture into storage neared, I walked off into the woods. My gloom followed me like a shadow. Not watching where I was going—just going, anywhere—I found a decaying log and sat down on it, my head falling into my lap, and cried out for help from all the powers I had ever heard of.

Sprinkles of rain rustled the carpet of leaves covering the forest floor. In the stillness, I felt a familiar presence, yet no one was around. Just a feeling, I thought. Then, my father came to mind. It was as if he were there, although I knew that to be impossible. He was dead.

I couldn't shake it; something seemed to be sitting beside me, shoulder to shoulder. Then I felt I was being hugged. A warmth passed through my body, even in the dank, early spring chill.

As the feeling passed, Lee Lyons, an Onondaga friend, came to mind. He had been an early champion of the article on the Iroquois and had died in a V.A. hospital while undergoing open-heart surgery during the coverage. I thought about how much of a friend he had become and what a loss I felt at his death. Then, just as quickly, my mind turned to what he had endured being an Indian. He had worked hard for the welfare of his people, and maintained a spirited attitude in the midst of monumental obstacles along his path. My problems paled in comparison.

My mind wandered. I floated back and forth between an awareness of the fragrances rising from the earth dampened by the light drizzle and the recollection of the beginnings of my involvement with Native Americans. The present and the past seemed to blur into a natural oneness.

"We learn only through experience. If we have no experiences, we won't know much. Have some, we may know a little—if we learned anything from them."

I was wet, soaked through. The drizzle had turned into a light rain. Drops of water fell rhythmically from drenched strands of hair drooping over my forehead. My clothes clung to my shivering body. Fragments of scenes came and went. An awareness of the past and present drifted in and out. Both were reality. Which was which? Reality and fantasy flowed together. I closed my eyes and wept. A dim memory of the past emerged.

My wife and I sat cross-legged in front of each other. The brass ashtray was in between, in the middle. We had no idea of what we were doing; an elder had given us instructions on how to carry out the ceremony. The elder had warned that we must be very careful. "Be very careful what you ask for," she had said, shaking a thin finger in my face. "Sooner or later you will get what you ask for, so get ready for it. It will be coming." Then she had eased back in her ragged, overstuffed chair, resting her head in the stuffing's groove. It was obvious she had thrown her head back into that position many times before. After a few minutes, she added, "May not be what you thought it was going to be, but it'll be yours. So be careful. Sometimes it's better not to ask for anything, but then, how do we learn how to ask?" She chuckled.

I knew what I was going for. The request was already in my mind as my wife put the sage in the ashtray. I took a match and lit it. The pungent odor, an aroma of the earth, spread quickly as stringent gray smoke streaked upward in occasional curls.

With our arms spread wide, forming a crescent, and our hands cupped toward our bodies, we scooped at the elusive vapor.

"Splash it, like splashing water, all over your body," the old Seneca had told me. "Start at the top of your head and gently go down your whole body. All the way to your toes," she had said. "It's for purification, cleansing. That's to open up the channel. Puts your mind in unity with the Creator. He hears what your thoughts are, your prayers. Keep them pure, though. Always give thanks, be thankful."

Closing her eyes, she had added, "Just one power. Be careful how you use it. Want only good to come back. It can be used to work bad. That comes back, too."

I vaguely heard B.J. giving thanks; my mind was deep into contemplation. Then it was my turn. After years of working with the elders, seeing their peace of mind and being aware of their contentment, I made what I thought was the most sacred request I could think of. I wanted wisdom.

When the object of my entreaty didn't drop from out of the sky, I soon forgot about our simple rite, and other things began to occupy my time. My world was soon turned upside down. Assignments from magazines were canceled, problems with the car had to be dealt with, we would have to move. It all came at once, and it would be months before life leveled out to any degree of normalcy.

Years later, Lumbee elder Vernon Cooper helped me put things into a perspective I could partially understand. "Life is a series of experiences," he had said. "We learn only through experience. If we have no experiences, we won't know much. Have some, we may know a little—if we learned anything from them.

"See this knot, here on my hand," Vernon pointed to a large lump near the base of his thumb, "that's what I got when I worked on a man with cancer. Had it real bad. Took it right out of his body. Took it in me. Had to. That was the only way I knew. Take it on myself to help him."

Leaning against his old car by the shed where he kept some of his herbs, he propped his walking stick between his legs as he carefully rubbed his aging frail hands together. "There's a better way, didn't know it at the time. You learn. Still I carry this with me. All these years. I can't ever forget."

Trudging back to the house, the cloud over me grew darker. I tiptoed across the deck, not wanting to announce to my family that I was brooding in the shadows.

I watched them through the sliding glass doors for a long time. What would it be like not to have them? I shuddered. What would it be like for them if I was not in the picture? The thought of my own death pricked me to the core of my soul. I shook my head, trying to dispel the possibility. Immediately, I was reminded of their love, and a sliver of light streaked downward into my dark pit. Although the thought of death lingered, a ray of hope had briefly appeared.

Chief Shenandoah's admonition flashed into my mind. "You got to work for the good. The bad will come on its own. It's just that way. It has always been that way."

Something moved, a shadow maybe, but I froze. My mind whirled. A terror grabbed me. Instantly it was as if I were seeing life from the other side, much like standing on the back side of a two-way mirror. I knew those I was watching were alive, I knew I was alive, but I was seeing as if I were dead. Already dead! Dead! But alive! Unable to pull myself out of the gravity dragging me deeper into a dark abyss.

The house had become my refuge. The terror of death struck every time I stepped outside. More and more I stayed holed up within the confines of my sanctuary.

Little by little my wife nudged me. "Just take your camera into the woods and take a few pictures," she gently pleaded. "I know it will be hard, but you'll see. It'll help."

One day, while she was at work, I followed her advice. To my surprise, it did feel good. Each time I went out, I ventured a little farther. Soon I was driving around, photographing scenes in different parts of the city. The emotional strings tying me to the house began to loosen.

Just as a measure of freedom from my gloom was emerging, I lost the house. The title holder didn't want to take it back, but he said he had no alternative: Payments had to be made. However, I could store the furniture in his warehouse for free until I found a house. He was sorry.

Traumatized, but without any alternative, we moved into a four-room apartment with a Lumbee Indian friend for several months. My wife and I had one bedroom, our friend had his, and our children—alternating between the sofa and the floor—took the living room. My depression continued.

Throughout the summer we huddled together, eventually realizing that although we had nothing materially we had each other. That was enough to sustain us.

In time a house was found to rent—no small feat when one's credit is destroyed—and we were reunited with our furniture. Conditions began to improve, but my gloom persisted. My self-esteem remained at a low. Any sense of my own self-worth was simply nonexistent.

Because my depression was literally sucking the life from those around me, I felt there was nothing left for me to do. I would have to take my own life. I calculated that by removing myself, I would give everyone else a chance to live.

One night, long after midnight and while everyone else slept, I slipped into my wife's and my bedroom. Ever so quietly, I eased across the room and carefully pulled out my .22 pistol from a dresser drawer. Returning to my tiny basement office, I shut the door and turned off the light. Blindly, I felt my way to my desk and crawled underneath. Curled into a ball and with gun in hand, I contemplated my next move. I began to cry uncontrollably, eventually falling asleep. Before long I awakened; the concrete floor had numbed my flesh. Struggling out from under the desk, I sat thinking for the rest of the night.

As the sun rose and light seeped into the room from under the door, I made my way upstairs and into my own bed—almost asleep before I slid between the covers.

Night after night, I would retreat to my dungeon. My despair was so deep that I would load and unload the gun over and over. The darkness was so black, and I moved within a fog so thick that I barely functioned. Yet, as the level of my affliction dropped, step by step, I prayed that if only I could hit the bottom, I could end it. Something prevented me, holding me in a purgatory. I was in a living hell, unable to end it all and yet afraid that I would.

I reached out for help from colleagues. To my surprise they cut me off. It was as if they were afraid of being associated with me, that I would drag them down.

During a brief conversation with a photographer friend, I was told, "Just get what the magazine wants, give the editors what they think they want. Pose the pictures, slant the take, do what is necessary. You'll be better off. You'll make money and get more work. On your own time you can go off and do whatever, you'll have the funds to do it. Better than starving." The discussion ended abruptly, and the phone went dead.

Through some invisible code, friends—Indian and non-Indian—began to call. They seemed to sense the trouble I was in. The Indians said they had seen it before. Years earlier, an Onondaga, Lee Lyons, before his death, had told me a story.

A non-Indian realized that the real history of the Indian people had not been fully told. He learned of the broken treaties, the duplicity on the part of the United States Government, the cholera-infected blankets given out to Indians by the army, and other atrocities committed against the Indians. He had discovered that the sacred wampum belts of the Iroquois had been taken illegally and ended up in museums. He tried to do something about it. He fought to get New York State to return the belts the state held. The state refused. The man was devastated. Many believed that had left him depressed and had, possibly, led to his death soon after.

"Don't take things too seriously," Lee had advised. "Just do what you think your duty is and let it go. A person can only do so much. Leave the rest to the Creator. It's how we have had to live. And still do."

I never imagined that I would discover so much and be so shocked by what I found. I was just not prepared for the stories of torture, of Indian corpses being rendered, of skeletons taken from graves and studied, of missionaries tying students' tongues with rubber bands if they even spoke their language.

The elders, in my meetings with them, had expressed forgiveness and were still eager to share their way of life with me, a white man. In spite of their people's tragic past, they spoke hopefully of the future, showed concern for the children of all races, and expressed their deep abiding love for the earth. Above all, they were able to laugh.

"We laugh," an elder said, "because that's what keeps us going. Stop laughing and you die. Maybe you should laugh more, too; it'll get you through the hard times."

As difficult as it was for me to see any hope, any light, any relief, I appreciated my friends' compassion. They were truly concerned and they were not afraid to show it.

I was told, "You may think you have lost everything, but when you can see you will know you have gained more than you ever had to give up. You will have found yourself. Some never do.

Although things had begun looking up for me professionally, by no means had I come to terms with the inner demons that still tormented me.

"When you can see, just give thanks for what you have gone through, what you are going through. Just give thanks. When you start doing that, things will change. Words have power."

Late one night, after everyone had gone to bed, I drifted down to my cramped office. Carefully, I pulled my gun out from my secret hiding place. Holding it, I stared at it for a long time. Slowly, I took the bullets out. Bowing my head for a long time, just letting different thoughts roll through my mind, I took a small screw driver from the desk drawer and, determined, started taking the .22 apart. In minutes, parts were everywhere. Then, rushing upstairs, I grabbed several garbage bags and tiptoed back to my office. Meticulously, I divided the springs, screws, handle, rotary, and barrel and threw everything into different bags so that no one, not even me, would ever be able to find enough of the jumbled pieces in the trash to put the gun back together. Then I took the bags out to the road for the garbage pickup the next morning. The gun was gone forever.

After that, things began to turn slowly around. It was as if my life, my soul, had hit bottom and was now starting to bounce back up. I was still on a roller coaster, but now each peak crested higher and higher, while the valleys were not as deep. I began to joke and let my laughing carry me over the downs. As I began to really care about others, instead of just myself, I proposed an article on the elders to *New Age Journal*. To my amazement, the editors waxed enthusiastic. They asked me to write the text, and it was published under the title "A Great and Undying Spirit." A glowing review appeared in *USA Today*. The editor of a small publishing company in Portland, Oregon, called a few days later and asked if I could make a book out of the material. I was floored. Make a book out of my unpublishable pictures of the elders!

I thought hard. Harvey Arden, I knew, still had the tapes of the interviews. He and I also had extensive notes and journals on the journey to the Grandfathers—the material for the article *National Geographic* had killed with such seeming finality.

I called Harvey about it and asked if he wanted to work together to produce a text for the book. His answer was a definite "Yes." Within weeks we signed a contract, and a year later, in 1990, the book came out as *Wisdomkeepers: Meetings with Native American Spiritual Elders*. It began to sell, and the modest royalties kept food in the mouths of my family.

Although things had begun looking up for me professionally, by no means had I come to terms with the inner demons that still tormented me. Yet, I had been encouraged enough by the interest in my work with the elders to test myself more. By ever so slightly pushing back the curtain of my despair, I resolved to continue my journey to the elders. I told myself it was not over; it was I who had invited the pause. The elders' spirituality still drew me. I wanted to know more. This time, however, there was no doubt as to what direction I would go in. It would be to the Indian women. A year later my book *Wisdom's Daughters: Conversations with Women Elders of Native America* was published by HarperCollins.

Harvey was on his own journey, as well. After taking early retirement from *National Geographic,* he had taken off for Australia to work with the aboriginal people of that country's vast outback.

As for me, I realized my road to recovery would be slow and painful. At times I was hardly aware of my inner darkness; at other times it blew over me like gale-force winds. Rebounding, however, became easier.

9

FACING THE DEMONS

I was in shock. All my plans had fallen through.

For months I had built the framework for continuing my journey to the Indian elders. I was drawn to them because I believed, rightly or wrongly, that they could give me the spiritual answers I couldn't find in my own culture. This time I carefully plotted my travels so that there would be no surprises. I was definitely going overland through Central and, possibly, South America. Years earlier, Native American patriarchs I had met in the United States had roused my interest. One, then another and another, in their own way, had gently pushed, saying, "Look to the south. There's something there."

I was ready for more. I knew I needed to hear what they had to say. I had not been able to bring a personal understanding to all I had heard. For me, something was missing. Maybe I was just looking for that one person who would wave some sort of magic wand to bring healing to my aching soul or lead me to a utopia of mental peace. Over the years, I had been finding real people willing to share the knowledge they had, but now I wanted even more. Exceptionally wise as they had been, I prodded on in my search. For what, I did not know. I believed that when I found it, I would recognize it.

Thinking I was smart enough to outwit my own terror, the fear of flying, I determined that I would drive the distance at whatever cost. I made my plans so clandestinely that no one could ever suspect my intentions.

I was like three people—the one before the depression, the one in the grip of it, and the one beyond it but still carrying some of the remnants.

Going to the southern elders was never in question. It was as if my itinerary were etched in stone. I knew the importance of the elders' words and the significance of the wisdom I would encounter. I had accepted the responsibility of whatever sacrifices such a pilgrimage would require. The only question in my mind was what mode of transportation I would have to endure. I staunchly maintained that flying would not be one of them.

I believed, the more I talked my travels up, that I could somehow bring the overland expedition off. I hoped to ensure the land route by inviting a close, personal friend to accompany me. Don Dahler, a fellow Charlottean at the time and an exceptional filmmaker who later joined CBS as a producer for "48 Hours," was ecstatic over the prospect. He readily accepted.

Together we left no stone unturned. Don studied vehicles for endurance and educated himself in survival techniques. I called manufacturers about the availability of four-wheel drives suitable for the trip. Meanwhile, he talked with mechanics about adding fuel tanks, mounting additional spare tires, and gathering together essential tools for the road. I called embassies about the requirements for crossing borders. He secured road maps for every country through which we would be traveling. I obtained metal cases for equipment. He ordered specialty items, such as mosquito nets, hammocks, and, just in case food was scarce, canned goods. Don accepted the task of arranging the packing.

Don's enthusiasm never waned, but at times I became overwhelmed. Inside, I trembled. I silently feared that something would cause the plan to collapse. I had never cowered prior to my plunge into depression. I tried to maintain face, but at every turn I remembered my descent and feared, if nothing else, the reemergence of its darkness. I was afraid the fear of its return would cause me to cringe.

I was like three people—the one before the depression, the one in the grip of it, and the one beyond it but still carrying some of the remnants. Part of me was still my old self. I could easily recall having logged over a half-million air

Despite my inner struggle, virtually a war within the confines of my mind that touched my every emotion, a powerful determination took command.

miles traveling the world and covering assignments in over forty countries. That I had written and photographed in areas of conflict such as Vietnam, Northern Ireland, Israel, and Lebanon. That was the same one who had been the journalist rushing in to report on political and natural disasters. There were earthquakes in Peru and Guatemala; hurricanes in Honduras, Florida, and Mississippi; and famine in India and Bangladesh. Then, I never felt the need to fear, believing I had a purpose. Everything had been possible.

In the gloom of my self-imposed captivity, I saw myself as a distorted, unworthy, and unlovable creature. Slowly, layers of my being, I was convinced all of them, had been stripped away. I had become, in my shattered mind, only a shadow of someone else. There was no more me.

Gradually I had begun to come back together until I felt at least partially resurrected. Now, a crisis was building anew, and my family was fully aware. They helped to hold me steady. But Don helped me build resolve, without knowing it, with his enthusiasm. I was still a believer, I had not lost that, but now he was the doer. Where I had waves of doubt, with Don on board, the trip was reality. He reminded me of my younger self.

In the end, our efforts were not enough to bring off the endeavor as it had been envisioned. As the plans began to fall through, and it was obvious that the vehicle could not be obtained and equipped in time, Don suggested we take his truck. It was a four-wheel drive. However, his Bronco developed engine trouble within days after his offer. It was decided that it would be risky, at the least, to take it. After all, it was seven years old and had almost 150,000 miles on the odometer.

Next, he pleaded, "We could change the date to leave. If I had a little more time, I believe we could work out the problem of getting a car and changing it to our specifications."

I had no choice. There was fate to contend with. Contacts had been made. Dates had been set. There were people waiting for my arrival. When I finally came to the conclusion and made what was, for me, the ultimate decision, I called Don, "We'll have to fly," I said. "It's come down to that."

No sound came from the receiver. I wanted to slam the phone down and run somewhere, anywhere. I didn't. I just waited for his response.

When his words—actually his word—did come, I interpreted the choking sounds as, "Wha . . . w-h-a-t!"

I said nothing, momentarily taking a perverse pleasure in his disbelief.

Catching his breath and forming his words into a complete sentence, he bellowed, "Hello? Who is this? I know it can't be who I think it is!"

"There's no other choice," I sighed. "I have to go—on schedule."

"This is great. It'll work. Let's do it."

"The more important the results, the more difficult the getting there will be. There are no breakthroughs without hard work and sacrifice. Discoveries only come from the edge."

Our focus shifted. Calls were made and faxes sent. A new itinerary was drawn up and airline tickets purchased. As details fell into place, I began to feel that with the completion of each phase I was driving another nail into my coffin.

As the days rapidly passed and departure neared, I grew more tense. I sensed the sanity I had slowly earned back slipping away. Despite my inner struggle, virtually a war within the confines of my mind that touched my every emotion, a powerful determination took command. I was not going to be seen as weak. I was going to make the journey, or at least die on it.

Then came the explosion, just after my internal truce had been reached. There was a glitch. Don would have to drive to San Antonio to drop off his dog, Skye, with his parents. It was decided he would take a flight from there and join me in Miami. I would have to fly the first leg of the trip to Costa Rica alone.

It was as if the gods were playing tricks on me, and I didn't like it. Suddenly, Leandis's words from my first conversations with him in the late 1970s flew out from somewhere in the back of my mind, "The more important the results, the more difficult the getting there will be. There are no breakthroughs without hard work and sacrifice. Discoveries only come from the edge."

Mustering courage, I put the finishing touches on my packing. As I drove to the airport, I saw little of the landscape. I was in a daze. At any moment, I knew I would crack. Talking to myself, I said, "I can't do this. I won't do this. I can change it. I can stop it. I'll cancel, and that'll be that."

Once in the terminal, my stride slowed. Each step became a chore. Over and over I told myself I could back out. Through the security check, I mumbled, oblivious to the stares. Waiting at the gate, my pulse increased and my temperature must have risen. I was hot.

In my inferno, the only word that could penetrate my cell was "flying."

Flying!

June 16, 1986, was the day I had told Harvey Arden that I had quit flying. Four years after that, because I had no choice, I had had to fly again. Harvey and I were traveling together, first to Portland to meet with the publisher of what would become *Wisdomkeepers,* then on to Phoenix where we rented a car for a drive to meet Hopi elders, and then back to Phoenix for the flight home the next day. To make sure we would not have to fight the rush-hour traffic the next morning, we had checked into a motel near the airport. All afternoon the building had shaken at closely timed intervals from the thunder of planes powering up then storming down the runway for takeoff.

I remember making an excuse that the room was stuffy and going out on the balcony to try to overcome my fear. I had been near the point of a panic attack. The next day I was going to have to fly again to get home. Vainly I tried to figure a way to get out of it. Nothing reasonable would come. Still in a semi-depression, the darkness would come and go, and I realized I had not been reasonable or even logical for a long time, and now I was even less so.

As I stood there sweating in the 110 degree heat, getting a nervous rush every time a plane sliced through the huge red-orange sphere of the sun on lift-off, it hit me. It was June 15, 1990. The next day would be June 16. June 16! Four years. The next day would be four years to the day since my last flight in a jetliner. Phoenix. Phoenix! I had been in Phoenix and now I was back in Phoenix.

I was petrified as I thought about the number four. As I recalled the meaning of four in Indian mythology—four being holy, the number for completion—I clutched the railing, cold beads of perspiration forming at my hairline and rolling down my forehead. Even the waistband of my pants became drenched as my heart pounded. Could it be that I had cheated death once and now I was back at the same place four—oh my God, four—years later to go through with my fate, whatever it was? And—it couldn't be true!—even the time of the flight seemed to be the same.

Like the reverberations of the planes above me, over and over I thought, "There are no coincidences. Sooner or later you get what you ask for. Be prepared."

I was quickly jolted back to 1993 by the loudspeaker at the Charlotte airport calling out the number 865. I felt sick. My flight had been called. I sat motionless. Everyone else lined up, marched down the ramp. I sat on.

The next thing I knew, my wife was tapping my arm. Her words were soft. "It's time to go." I looked around. We were the only ones left in the boarding area. It was now or never, I thought, and I entertained the idea of never. B.J. must have read my mind. "You've got to do it. You know you'll be all right. You're protected just like all the other times. This is your new beginning. Look at it like that."

Getting out of the seat was one of the hardest things I had ever done, but I managed to stand. Blood rushed to my head, and I felt faint. Tenderly I kissed my wife and held on to her for dear life. Taking too much time, she pushed me away and pointed to the exit.

"I'll see you," I whispered, "I won't say good-bye, that's too final." Holding back the tears, I blubbered, "I'm coming back, you know?"

She hugged me, again, and whispered, "That's already a fact. That's not a question. Turn it around. Make it a statement. And, yes, you will!"

B.J. pulled away, and I inched down the ramp. With my fingers outstretched, I marked an invisible line along the wall. I couldn't look back. If I did, I knew that I would run to her, grab her hand, and drag her back to the car.

Pausing at the entrance, I inhaled deeply. Once, twice, three times. Then, I gasped. I was lighted-headed; I had overdone it. When I recovered from the oxygen overdose, I was nearly to the door of the plane and thankful no one saw my antics. Any observer would have sworn I was intoxicated.

Soon the monstrous machine was being pushed backward. Seeing my wife at the huge glass window of the terminal, I held a piece of white paper to my window in hopes she would know it was me. But she gave no indication she saw it, and that saddened me even more.

Rolling to a stop at the end of the runway, I knew the time had come. This was it. After pulling my belt tighter, I held on to the arms of my seat for takeoff.

Clasping his hands together, fingers intertwining, he looked at me with a strained intensity and said, "I think I'm going to die on this trip."

Just as we gained speed, I laughed. I thought, you're crazy. What good will holding on do?

I let go and relaxed, letting whatever would come come. What happened was the return of an old and thrilling sensation. I had always loved the takeoff; I had always loved flying. But I checked the feeling, allowing the familiar fear to take over. I was back in terror.

In an attempt to console myself, I thought about my family. Immediately, I was comforted. B.J. was not just my wife, never had been. She was my partner. Her love had carried me through when I was unlovable. I whispered a "thank you" as I thought about all that I had put her through over the years.

Lisa, my daughter, had called just before I left to tell me how much she loved me. She had said that we would do something special together when I returned.

Chris, on the other hand, I recalled, had not said much. Hugging me as I went out the door, he had slipped an envelope into my pocket. The envelope!

Now I frantically rummaged for it, finally finding it in the last possible place. I tore it open and read it.

Chris had penned, "I wanted to tell you that I love you very much. It will not be easy on me while you are gone. I will miss you, but I know that you will be back soon."

Water filled my eyes, blurring my vision as I tried to look out the window in a vain attempt to pick out landmarks below and divert my attention from my aching heart, now lodged precisely in my throat. Composing myself, I went back to the letter.

"You are a very talented person. I envy you your intelligence and your wisdom."

I had to fold the handwritten note and close my eyes tight, squeezing my face into a deformed crush of deep furrows. Both of my children had told me often that they loved me and had shown it in so many ways, but Chris had always carried his emotions deep inside. Now he was letting me know how he felt about me. A letter was a safe place to do it. That was okay with me; that he was doing it at all was enough. I soared, as any parent would at such an admission.

For some time I just held the missive delicately with both hands in front of me. I gazed intently at the three printed letters, "Dad," on the envelope. Then, I reopened it to finish reading.

"I wish that I could be with you right now. You will be with me in my mind all the time. I will be thinking, 'I wonder where he is right now, and what is he doing.'

"Call me at any time of the day or night and let me know how you are. You could also write to me.

"I miss you, Dad, and I love you very, very much. You will be all right. I just know it!

"I love you, Chris."

During the rest of the flight, I thought about the three of them and read Chris's letter four times. I was at peace in their love, because, I thought, if love is the most powerful force in the world, I am protected.

Things changed in Miami. As soon as I landed and claimed my baggage, I headed to the Lacsa Airline counter. The attendant was wonderful. Although Don had not arrived, she checked both of us in, assigned our seats, and tagged my luggage.

Grabbing a cup of coffee, I walked from one end of the terminal to the other to meet Don at his gate. As the passengers disembarked, there was no Don. I stood impatiently, in case he was going to end up being the last one off. When the airline agent came out and locked the door, I realized something was wrong. Everyone was out.

I rushed to the ticket counter to inquire as to whether he had missed his flight or if something had happened. If something had happened to the plane. . . . I quizzed the representative. "No," he said, "the plane is on time. The passengers have all deplaned."

Don wasn't on the flight. I knew something had gone terribly wrong. In great leaps, I rushed to find a phone and call my travel agent in Charlotte to see if he could find out anything. Guy Crowe checked as best he could and determined that Don must have taken another flight, because he had missed his connection. I was only slightly relieved when he added, "There haven't been any disasters. You know what I mean. I'm sure nothing serious has happened."

Still, I was in shock. As a dull pain hit the bottom of my stomach, I heard my name being called out over the loud speaker, "Mr. Steve Wall. Pick up the white service phone, please. Mr. Wall, pick up any white service phone."

Running to an information desk, I grabbed a phone and waited. No one responded. I waited impatiently. Nothing. I began to sweat, thinking that whoever was trying to contact me would not wait long. In a panic, I considered flinging down the damn white courtesy phone and charging to a pay booth to call home to find out if anything had happened. Finally, in desperation I asked the specialist at the information counter for help. I was politely directed to another "working" phone.

"I'll put you through," the voice at the other end said after I introduced myself.

"Hello," came an all-too-familiar voice.

"Hello," I said, shaking, knowing that something was very wrong.

"Steve, this is Sara James."

I knew immediately it was Don's wife, a correspondent with NBC News. I froze. Only if something terrible had happened would she be calling me in the Miami airport. Don would never have missed this trip, not this one.

"Yes, Sara. For God's sake, what has happened?"

"Everything is fine. Don's all right. There was a problem with his plane, causing a delay. He missed his connection because of it. He got another flight, but he won't be able to get there in time for your Lacsa flight to Costa Rica."

I was relieved. Don was alive.

"He called me on the phone in the plane. He's in the air now. He said you could wait for him and you two could take the flight tomorrow, or, if you want, you could go on. He'll meet you there tomorrow."

She paused, waiting for an answer. Neither of us said anything. Silence. I was in no condition to make a decision. My head was spinning. Fate was involved, I knew, as I grappled with these late and enormous problems I had been confronted with. Maybe I was being saved by having to wait for him, I wrestled with myself. Maybe I was supposed to be on the flight alone, maybe it was Don's flight that would have a problem.

"I'm going on," I said. "Tell Don I'm supposed to be on this flight. Tell him, if he calls you, I'll see him in Costa Rica. I have to go on," and I stuttered, "f—fo—for some rea—reason." And she was gone.

I was not entertained by the chain of events. Leg one by myself. Now, leg two alone. I felt like the pawn in some sort of high stakes game. There appeared to be a ruling force in control, and I was not just in the contest; I felt I was the sport.

I was in agony as I boarded yet another flight. The sinking sensation was back. "How ridiculous you are," I told myself, trying to reason. Fear had become a tyrant, and now I yearned for the wanderer within to return.

The trip to Costa Rica, the first stop of my Central American tour, had gone smoothly. The liftoff had been exhilarating. And the artistry of the pilot had been inspiring. I didn't even know when the wheels left the ground, and when the gigantic craft touched down, it was a three-point landing.

The next day when I went back to the airport to meet Don, I was two hours early. I was shaky. My flight had been without so much as a bump. Now I waited to see what fate would deliver, praying that my emotional rantings were unfounded.

They were. Don arrived safely. However, that night in the hotel room, with photographic equipment, tape recorders, clothes, canteens, and bags strewn everywhere, we talked. He grew serious as he sorted through the mess. I was not accustomed to this side of him, and it caught me off guard.

Stopping what I was doing to sit on the side of the bed, he did the same thing. Clasping his hands together, fingers intertwining, he looked at me with a strained intensity and said, "I think I'm going to die on this trip."

Wait a minute, this is wrong, I thought. I wanted to get away from him. I couldn't handle the idea of death. It had stalked me too long.

In a flash, I was standing, searching for a way to make some excuse, any pretext, to get out of the conversation. I sat back down, he was in earnest, and I tried to joke, "Well, shit, let me know where and when, so I won't be there when you croak. I don't know what the 'unknown' is, but I am not ready for it, and I'm not ready to be around it if you're going."

"Hey, don't get me wrong. I'm not afraid of it. It doesn't bother me in the least. Actually, I'm kind of looking forward to it. It's just another journey. It'll be an adventure."

I sat straight up, rigid. "I don't want any part of it," my voice going as bass as it could. "No, no way. Not me. Let's stop this conversation. Let's stop it now."

"All I'm saying is that I think I'm going to die on this trip. It's just a feeling. If it happens, it happens."

"Let's go get a drink. Get out of here!"

"That sounds good, but I still mean what I'm saying."

Trying to project anger instead of yielding to my bubbling hysteria, I frowned, my jaw locking. "Look! Get this straight. You may think you're going to die, but it just might be that a part of you has to die because of what you're going to learn. All that means is that another part of you is going to be born."

Here I was giving a lecture as if I knew what I was talking about, some sort of sage. The words were the truth, but I was the last person who should have been delivering them. Then, it dawned on me. The words were for me.

Don laid back, his hands behind his head, and said, "You're right. That's what that must be. Let's go have a drink."

10

HIGH PRIESTS AT THE CENTER OF THE WORLD

I was late arriving at the "Center of the World." The Jawa, or Cabecar, high priests, were already there and waiting for other lowlanders bringing gifts of used clothing for the Costa Rican Cabecar Indian children. Although my torturous sixty-five-mile journey by four-wheel drive over the Central Mountains into Chiripo had taken more than five hours, it didn't compare to the trek of the two medicine men.

Making their way over trails even too precarious for horses to pass, the brothers had started the day before from their lofty compounds high in the jagged, towering mountains. Leaving from different passes, where distance is measured in walking time, they had each spent the night alone in the clouds shrouding the damp forests. Rising well before the sun, each began to complete the remainder of his fast-paced ten-hour walk. They had reached the narrow, elevated plateau where the Cabecar community of Grano de Oro lay at mid-morning.

Hermenegildo and Tomas Aguilar waited out of the way, off to one side of the main entrance, as their people slowly congregated. The group, hardly filling the community's central meeting hall, came for the gathering the Aguilars were to preside over. As members of the Utsekar clan, the clan of the healers, they neither projected an air of authority nor showed any impatience. From the time they were children, they had been taught to listen to Utsekar, the special spirit of the Jawa whose name means "The God That Commands Them."

Bent from the weariness of their laborious travels and with the lack of sleep showing in their bloodshot eyes, they greeted me warmly. Other non-Indians

"We don't understand why there are
those who would destroy the land.
That is the same as destroying our life.
Would anyone destroy his own mother?"

pulled to a stop just beyond the barbed-wire fence at our backs and began carrying several cardboard boxes from their car into the building.

"Could I talk with you later?" I asked, feeling too pushy even as the question came out of my mouth. Nevertheless, I went on, "I'd like to talk about God."

"You're here about God?" Tomas responded, looking at me in surprise. Bowing as he eased away to go inside, he added, "When the gathering is over, there are things to talk about."

By the time Hermenegildo and Tomas crossed the center's dusty concrete floor, the white woman had dragged a chair into the middle of the room and hurriedly arranged the used clothes next to it. She sat down facing the reticent villagers, who were suspiciously eyeing her. As the Jawapa took their seats on a bench in the back, the crowd grew quiet. Through an unspoken signal, the nod was given to begin.

As each piece of clothing was individually pulled from the box and held up, one child after another was coaxed to stand in front of the woman for a fitting. One by one, first a boy, then a girl, bashfully half–stepped up to be measured. With the sizing complete, each child, without being permitted a choice, received the garment and returned to join other family members. In less than an hour all the clothes had been given away, leaving disappointment on the faces of some of the children.

I felt dismayed over what I had witnessed. Although it had nothing to do with me, I was confused. There had not been enough clothes to go around. Of the fortunate few who did manage to fit into a shirt, pair of pants, or a dress, no one had been allowed to personally select it. The choice had been made for them. Then, I asked myself, "Is this all there is to the gathering the Jawa walked ten hours to attend?"

Having seen enough, I decided to go outside and have a smoke. As I walked around, thinking the gathering would go on for a long time, I marveled at the beauty of the place. Although the people appeared to be poor, I quickly recognized that they were living in a virtual paradise. Too bad, I reasoned, that bartering was vanishing; otherwise the people would have no need to change their ways just to get a hold of cash to obtain the goods they needed.

Within a half-hour, people began coming out of the building. Like at a family reunion, people gathered in clusters to talk and laugh. Kids ran from group to group, while others loaded their pack horses for a return into the mountains. I made my way over to join Tomas, his brother, and their families. Although it was difficult communicating through an interpreter, we slowly began to become free enough, in spite of the barrier, to talk from the heart.

"Could you tell me about God?" I asked once again.

Tomas frowned, apparently trying to put his thoughts into words. Then, he said, "God is hard to explain. Maybe God cannot be explained. If I tell you some things, it may help."

Care of the Land

We are all one people throughout the whole world. This is our center, the center of the world for us. We do not destroy land because the land is where the herbs are to help us to cure people. The land is our mother. She's part of God, and we care for her just as we care for our human mother. Both are sacred for us.

The land gives us our medicine, gives us our life. We don't understand why there are those who would destroy the land. That is the same as destroying our life. Would anyone destroy his own mother?

We see, we watch, we know. That's part of our special training. The lessons are hard, but in them we are taught how to communicate with all of life. Because God is in all those things, we get close to Him.

It is unfortunate that there are people who went wrong. Their mentality directs their vision to material things like gold, mining, and building big buildings, and they don't give respect for nature. That's why they went wrong. Now they just go searching for material things. The Jawa place no value in those things.

We know it is important to take care of nature, because we understand that nature is life. To know this is the beginning of understanding God. It is our hope that people will change and begin to have respect for nature. If they do this, then they will change again into good people.

When we gather the herbs, we talk to them as we pull them up from the land. We take them into our hands, and we know that inside the herb is a good spirit. The plants have a spirit, a good spirit, and we talk to them. We know the good spirit will help us with our families and with the people we are going to cure. The good spirit will take out the illnesses that the people have inside their bodies. When we use the herb, we know we are carrying the good spirit that will help us and the people who receive it.

There are many people who have lost their way. They don't understand spiritual things. We know that evil spirits are inside the person who is sick. The herb will help them. So many look at the plants and see only grass and weeds. They are blind. They have made themselves blind and closed themselves off from their connection with God.

We know every person has a spirit inside of them. Some don't even know they are spirit. They don't have a spiritual feeling about themselves or about the things around them. It will be very difficult for others to relearn this spiritual feeling. For us, we know that each indigenous group has its own knowledge of the world around them and that knowledge is transmitted from each generation. Each nation or group has its different knowledge, so it would be very difficult to really teach other people this spiritual feeling. They have no foundation to relearn from, no past generations who

handed it down. The knowledge has been lost and there is no basis of understanding the spiritual feeling or of knowing God in this special way.

We live in the center, everything is a circle and we are part of it. Life is a circle. Life is the ceremony. It is lived every minute of every day. Because of that, there is no word in Cabecar for ceremony. It cannot be put into a word that could explain it.

Tomas's words were simple and profound. As the two of us stood silently looking at each other, I thought that if only I could speak his language and hear more, maybe I would be able to understand better. My inner self begged me to speak up, but nothing, not even a grunt, would come out of my mouth.

He waited.

Secretly I knew that his continuing was being left up to me. When he finally began to pull away because of my reluctance, I realized he had said all that he was going to say. Foolishly I had let the moment pass.

I said little as Don drove us out of the Cabecar village. Then, realizing that nothing is really ever lost, I turned around to Jose Julio Morales Martinez, a brilliant young Cabecar who had traveled into Grano de Oro with us and who was going with us back down the mountain. "Jose Julio!" I excitedly spoke up, just a little too loudly. "You introduced us to your grandmother. You said she knew so much of the spiritual ways. Do you think I could see her again? Do you think she would talk with me?"

Taken aback by my abruptness, he had to think for a moment. Then, he said, "Yes. Yes, if she hasn't gone home. It would be a long walk, if she has. That'd take many hours climbing up the mountain. And, we couldn't get there by car. There are no roads. She may still be visiting relatives in Jicotea, Platanillo."

As we dropped downward, rounding one hairpin curve after another and, at times, sliding seemingly on air above sheer cliffs, I prayed. Although occasionally my heart would lodge in my throat and my feet would tingle with each sudden dip, I surprised myself by feeling no fear. I had only one hope on my mind, that of being able to talk with Clementina Martinez.

Finally, we slowed to a stop. We had arrived in the hollow where Clementina Martinez had been visiting earlier in the day. She was nowhere to be seen. My hopes sank. Jose Julio decided to try one last possibility. Pointing the way, he gave directions up another road that looked like the one we had just come down. Quickly, however, it narrowed into a path and we parked.

HIGH PRIESTS AT THE
CENTER OF THE WORLD

Jose Julio raised his hand for me to wait as he checked to see if his grand-mother was inside the caretaker's quarters of the old sugar mill. Within a few minutes he returned and invited me in. Clementina Martinez would talk with me; she had not gone home.

Sibu

The name for God in my language is Sibu, the word meaning Supreme Master or the highest chief. Sibu came before all other things. So, before there was this land, when Sibu created this world, the only thing that you could see were rocks, rocks, and more rocks. Imagine all the mountains made out of rocks. Then, God decided to make the land, to create the mountains, the trees, and everything else in nature. After the land was made from rocks, humans and all living creatures appeared. The human was made from mud, a special type of mud. God modeled it from his own appearance as he thought he looked. God made the human from the mud and he gave life to it because of his spiritual feeling and, also, because of his power. He gave this piece of mud the property of life.

Sibu is taught to all the people so that each one can communicate with him for themselves. Therefore, Sibu is for everyone. He is not reserved for just a few. So the way to communicate is taught to everyone. We believe that all the things around the people here means Sibu, so you don't have to pray to Sibu because He is present in everything you see. Sibu is in all things.

There is an evil spirit that tries to keep the people away from Sibu. This would mean the same as devil in Spanish. This spirit is like a ghost, because you can't see it, but it's always present.

After Death

When someone dies we have special rites. There is not a word in Cabecar for ceremony, but rituals are made so that the spirit will return to Sibu. We make this ritual each year after the person has died to continue to release the spirit, because it will not always stay in one place here. It can pass from one side to the other. In other words, it travels. The rituals help to keep the spirit with Sibu, so that it will not have the need to cross over as much.

If you are not Cabecar, when you die you will still go to Sibu. There is no difference in God, just like all people are equal, God is equal, too. Everyone goes to only one place.

For our rituals, we burn wood. The fire will send our messages to Sibu. The smoke goes out and up into the air, and since Sibu is in everything, what we say to Him is received.

Sibu has never been angry, but if there is a time when He just gets fed up with the things that humans do, he could become very angry. Because He has the power, He could kill everybody.

11

THE WITCH WHO FLEW

The bull was on a rampage along the narrow hilly footpaths of the tiny community of Rey Curre. For three days the conflict had raged between the villagers, disguised under grotesque wooden masks, and the horned, burlap-covered bull. Old men and boys blew conch shells and horns as fellow tribe members joined an ever-increasing procession of combatants.

Now the entire hillside town lay under a suffocating layer of red-brown dust stirred up by flying arms, legs, and bodies locked head-to-head in combat with the powerful beast. Having moved with a mock, ceremonial viciousness from house to house—leaving no family untouched and pausing only long enough for the combatants to consume more and more alcoholic chicha—the ceremonial battle neared its end.

As the raging sun beat down and the stifling February heat rose to perilous highs, the exhausted Bruncas, their bodies bruised and covered with sweat and grime, lay as if dead. Pawing the ground, the pompous creature could now think he had been victorious. But the war was far from being over.

In the cool of the uneasy night following the slaughter, according to legend, the dead arose and reenacted the death battle in this tragic drama, clashing again and again with the symbolic bull. This year, as in each since the invasion of the Spanish colonists half a millennium ago, the Indians return as the "little evils." In the Brunca Feast of Kabruk, those ancient Indians are immortalized and continue to torment the descendants of those original colonists.

Having been invited to witness the Feast of the Little Evils in Rey Curre, I had rushed to leave the Brunca capital of Boruca in order to participate in the

109

last day's rituals of the feast. The sun was already center sky when I finished packing my gear and said my good-byes. I had hated to leave, since I had lived for days with seventy-eight-year-old Braulio Morales and his seventy-two-year-old wife, Celina. I had grown quite fond of them and the other elders there. Their remote mountain hamlet was the only home they had ever known. It was little wonder they never had any desire to leave.

My visit with them had been a good one. Day and night overlapped in the mountains of the elders.

I remembered awakening at the beginning of my first day, just as the dark was beginning to lift, and hearing the sounds of dawn long before the full light of the morning reached the dirt streets. Just beyond my open window I could smell sweet fragrances of tree-rippening oranges drifting in on the cool gentle breezes and hear horse hooves thumping in cadence up the winding lane. A mare snorted; its colt whinnied, the sounds of its tiny running feet tinkling like piano notes in response to a heavy cord. Competing roosters crowed, dogs barked, children laughed while chasing a loose pig.

In the late afternoon, after work in the steep fields high above the village had been completed, I would find the mood had shifted. As the shadow of the sun crept into the folds of the hills, a signal of the approaching dark, Braulio would drag one of the few chairs from his house, cross the concrete porch, and position himself squarely in the yard.

Night fell early under the mountains. Activity in the streets increased. People moved about, talking. Then everyone would begin to saunter home. Voices turned to whispers. Soon the silence drifted, like a wave, over the Brunca's isolated homeland. The village was about to go to sleep, but not Braulio.

Earlier, before the spreading quiet, his grandson had asked him to tell of the witches. With a "wait a while" frown, Braulio had responded with lowered voice, "Too many people. Too many ears. Wait. I will, but wait."

Waiting out in the night air, in anticipation of the stories, had been difficult for me. I was constantly fighting off the mosquitoes, slapping my already red-splotched body each time I felt anything at all. But I was patient as I had thought this particular night a good one for witch stories.

Just as the reclining crescent moon slowly mounted the jagged peaks encircling the settlement and came into full view, Braulio had seemed ready to talk. First, he let me know, there were other things he wanted to say.

Holding his index finger up to his lips, then pointing it at one of his ears and quickly twirling it around, his own form of sign language, he then whispered, "The voice carries, too many ears in the village. After everybody goes to bed and goes to sleep, they won't hear. I'll tell you this first, then about witches."

What You've Done, You Will Receive

What you have done in life, you receive from life. The stick you measure with is the stick you will be measured by. I have seen that. Here I have seen people who killed and were themselves killed the same way.

A Turkish man here had a grocery. He was a trader, and he was killed because he had money. One man hit him in the head with a hammer, and another stuck him in the chest with a knife. A woman friend hid the killers, and even made coffee for them. The next day they began to regret what they had done, but it was too late.

Soon people started asking about the grocer, because he was missing. It was never like him not to show up, but everyone said he was a trader. Probably, they tried to reason, he was just off somewhere.

One of the killers started asking about him to try to cover his actions.

By the second day, the same killer started casting blame toward another man. He suggested someone should check the trader's house. When everyone went to the house, he ran to a window and said, "Look! Thieves must have gone through the window."

The rural guards were present and they found the body. He had been hit on the head and stabbed in the heart with a knife. They called for an autopsy.

Because of this one man's actions, they suspected him and put him in jail. He got so afraid, he made a confession and admitted what he had done.

The other man could not be found, but the woman who helped was also sent to jail. After some time, the killer escaped from jail and fled to the mountains. One day he was cutting trees with an ax, and the trunk of the tree fell and broke his leg. Although he was still a fugitive, he had gained the trust of the people in the new community because they didn't know about his past. So the villagers took him to a doctor, but by the time they got him to the city, he was dead.

What you do in life will be returned. It will bounce back on you. When you do good, good will come to you.

"The witch was from a family that knew how
to transform themselves. She could change
into a reindeer."

When Braulio finished his story, he sat quietly for a few minutes. I could see that he was hesitating. His grandson, who sat next to him, coaxed him to continue. Soon Braulio began telling witch stories.

Witch Stories

There was this witch who lived on the Pacific coast who could fly. She waited every night for her husband to fall asleep. Then, she would fly to Panama. When her husband would wake up, she wouldn't be in the bed with him. Although he was a witch too but not as high of a one, he wouldn't know where she had gone.

This witch woman would leave her house every night about 11 P.M. Before she left, she would prick her husband's fingers to see if he was asleep.

One night her husband made himself appear as if he were sleeping. He felt her prick his fingers, but he didn't move. Then, after she left, he followed her to the nearby woods and saw her disappear.

This happened several times, and each time, he was careful to stay out of sight. Each time, after she disappeared, all that would be left would be her clothes. Apparently her family members would have clothes ready for her in Panama. They were witches, too. For me, I don't know how she could fly.

One night her husband followed her to the woods, got her clothes, and put salt on them. Then he went back home to sleep. When his wife returned, she couldn't put her clothes on. The salt did something. About 4 A.M. he heard a woman crying outside of the house, and he knew immediately it was his wife screaming and moaning, "Oh, my husband, why did you put salt on my clothes? Why have you done this to me?"

Acting like an innocent person, he jumped out of bed shouting, "Who is it? What is wrong?"

She kept on crying and went back into the woods naked. She said, "Why salt on my clothes?"

Early the next morning she asked again, "Why do you do this to me? Why?"

He answered, "Where have you been? I saw you disappear into the night."

Then she confessed, "I go to visit my family in Panama. My mother, my sisters."

"How long does it take?" he asked.

"Oh, not so much time. Now that you found me out, do you want to go with me?"

"If you can take me," he replied.

"I can't take you tomorrow, it is just impossible, because I have to tell my family first. Then, I have to get your measurements for clothes, because you will have to travel naked and put the clothes on when you arrive in Panama." Continuing on, she said, "I have to warn you. On the trip there is a lot of static, like thunder. Because of this static, it will be dangerous. You cannot say, 'Oh my God,' or you will fall. You won't die, the spirits will protect you, but they cannot keep you flying. If you say 'Oh my God,' they lose some of their power."

On the day they planned the trip, there was a feast with lots of guitars and singing. After the feast the husband started the journey with his wife. During the trip, the husband forgot and cried, "Oh my God," and fell.

The woman went on to Panama and told her family her husband had fallen because he said the words. Her family knew he was not dead. They knew he had fallen into a creek, and the spirits had broken his fall.

She returned to her husband and rescued him. The spirits told her, "Next time it will be impossible for him to do this because of static. He will say the words again and fall again. This time he will kill himself."

Still, she agreed to let him try again.

He told her, "Now I know where you go. I don't want to try again."

I went with Ponciano, my friend, to meet the witch woman. He had a lot of pain in his leg, so he went to the woman to see if she could heal the problem. It was well known that she cured some things but she couldn't cure Ponciano's leg. It was not long after that Ponciano died. He could never be cured, but that's another story.

The Reindeer Witch

There was a witch who lived near here who was a Bruja. She was very powerful and could change shapes. Nobody in this place knew about witches living here, but I knew.

This man had a bean field that was fenced in. He was growing summer beans, and he was careful to keep careful watch over his crop.

The witch was from a family that knew how to transform themselves. She could change into a reindeer. Because of a feud, this family was fighting the family of the man with the beans. So, she would become a reindeer and would come every day and eat beans all day long.

One day the man saw this reindeer jump his fence and eat his beans. He got his rifle and waited just long enough for her to jump back over the fence and shot. He missed.

On the next day the deer came back. He got his rifle and again tried to shoot her, but he didn't hit her. By now the bean field was about to be lost.

On the third day he was desperate. He had not been able to kill the reindeer. Again, he got his rifle, but he thought he was out of bullets. Bullets were scarce and he had wasted two. Finally, he found a bullet. Yes! A bullet. He got it, chewed on it for good luck, and went to the field. The deer was really entertained. This time he shot and hit the deer. The

"I have to warn you. On the trip there is a lot of static, like thunder. Because of this static, it will be dangerous. You cannot say, 'Oh my God,' or you will fall."

deer fell, then tried to jump, like being thrown. She tried to jump again. She jumped the third time and made it.

By now she was bleeding a lot, so he followed her trail. When he got to the road, he looked and the deer was walking along the side.

He thought, "How strange. Deer are supposed to run into the woods and this deer keeps to the road."

He tried to follow, but stopped about eighty meters from the house of this family when the deer went into the house. Soon he heard people crying and a young girl screaming in pain.

Some days later he heard that a relative of the family had died because of a bullet.

The brothers of the girl were very angry with the man who shot their sister. They approached him and he told them he shot a deer, not a woman. "It was a deer that I shot," he protested.

Some time later, there was a feast. One of the brothers saw the man who owned the beans and started a fight. Another brother came with a gun and shot the man to death.

There were a lot of people who saw this. The authorities came. People identified the brother as the killer, so they put him in jail. Finally, he admitted he killed the man for killing his sister.

THE WITCH WHO FLEW

His mother, also a witch, came to jail with food and told her son of a plan to get him out. On a night some prisoners were being transferred, she helped him break out of jail. She could do this because she was invisible. She simply took him on her shoulders and flew away.

Because of that, now everyone knows a woman can transform. Women witches have more power. They can transform into many different things. Witches can also invoke the evil spirits. Men usually can't transform or fly.

The Story of Tatica

Tica in Spanish means like God. It can also mean like a grandfather, and would be used as a sign of respect and affection.

My grandmother told me that Tatica Kuasran was this man that left when the conquerors came during the time of the colonization. Many of the Indian people left because they didn't want to be killed by the Spaniards.

Tatica depended on witch doctors because he was part of a special clan that depended on them. One of these witch doctors told him, "You must leave. The Spaniards are coming and they will kill you."

So Tatica went to the mountain and was able to transform himself into a spirit. But he always came back to the village because he had a lover here. When he came here, he looked like a normal person. He had his lover and they had a child together. The grandmother of my mother told me that Tatica said, "I'm going to take my child to the mountain."

He was asked, "How are you going to take him?"

"Well, you're going to see how I'm going to take him," he replied.

And he did take him to the mountain. The child was playing here one moment, then there came a strong wind and he was gone. It was Tatica who came and transformed himself into like a small hurricane and took the child with him. The child's name was Shascragua.

When this child grew up to be a young person, his father gave him his own territory in the highest part of the mountain. Tatica lived on one side of the mountain and his son lived over the mountain. They had their own dominion, their own territories.

Ponciano's Pigs

One day my friend Ponciano bought two pigs. They were very nice pigs, because they didn't have very much hair on their skin. Everyday the pigs left the house to search for food. Every day they would go further away and return later in the night or the next day. Then one day they just didn't return.

Ponciano decided to ask a sukia for help. He traveled here to see if the sukia could tell him if the pigs were still alive or dead, if they had been eaten by a tiger or if they had just been lost on the mountain.

The sukia told Ponciano to come back the next day. The next day the sukia told Ponciano, "Yes, the pigs are still alive but Titica Kuasran has them. Ponciano asked the sukia if he could use his power to make his pigs return to his house and offerred to pay him to do it.

The sukia just told him, "No need. I'll just tell you what I find out."

Ponciano returned two days later and was told that Tatica Kuasran did have his pigs and would return them on one condition. When the pigs were returned he would have to immediately kill them because if they escaped again Tatica would not return them again.

The sukia told Ponciano that Kuasran had told him that the pigs would be returning on Friday at about 8 P.M. and to be ready to close the fence when they were inside.

Ponciano prepared himself that night with wax candles, because in those times there was no electricity. They knew the pigs were coming because the other pigs were like getting restless. They were ready with matches to light the candles at just the right moment.

While they were waiting in the night, they heard the pigs. One of the old men with Ponciano ran, without being able to see anything in the night, and closed the gate without knowing if the pigs were inside or outside. When they thought they had the pigs they lit the candles and saw that the pigs were inside the fence.

The next day they were all happy and went out to see the pigs. Then, Ponciano decided he was not going to kill the pigs. "They're very good pigs," he said. "They have appeared and I have just bought them. So, I'm not going to kill them. No way, I'm not going to kill these two pretty pigs. I'm going to leave them right as they are."

So Ponciano sat about to tame the pigs. He let them come inside the house and stay with his family. They became such tame pigs, they allowed themselves to be touched. Ponciano's family was very trusting of the pigs. They let them go out and be with the other pigs. Some days they would let the pigs sleep with the other pigs and the next day come back into the house.

Soon they would let the pigs eat around outside and let them go to a nearby island in the river.

That night the pigs came back to the house and slept with the other pigs. On the next day Ponciano's family let the pigs go where they wanted again. So the pigs went to this same island, but they went on the other side of the island. The family tried to follow them into a savannah, but the pigs just disappeared. They didn't return on that night or the next day.

Ponciano's family was very desperate to find the pigs. Because they were so desperate Ponciano went again to the same sukia and he told him the pigs had disappeared. The sukia said, "Well, you didn't follow my instructions. I told you that it was better to eat them or give away the pigs."

Ponciano said, "I didn't kill them, because the pigs were so tame. They were beautiful pigs and now they're gone. But, if you make me another favor, I will be grateful to you, if you could try to make the pigs come again. This time I will kill them."

The sukia told him, "Well, I will see. I'm going to try to see if I can get your pigs to come again."

Ponciano came back the next day and the sukia told him, "Well, I went to see Tatica Kuasran. Tatica is very angry. He's not going to return the pigs, because you disobeyed his orders. You didn't follow the instructions. It doesn't matter if you offer a lot of money, he's not going to return the pigs. You didn't follow the instructions."

The pigs didn't ever return. Ponciano told me this story in 1931 about the pigs. The sukia told Ponciano that Tatica Kuasran had many animals on his mountain. But no one would enter to take his animals.

For disobeying, Ponciano was told by the sukia he would get an incurable disease. The sukia said, "I'm not going to tell you what the illness will be, because I don't want you to be afraid when you get it."

Ponciano lived about one year after that. He died from chronic asthsma.

THE WITCH WHO FLEW

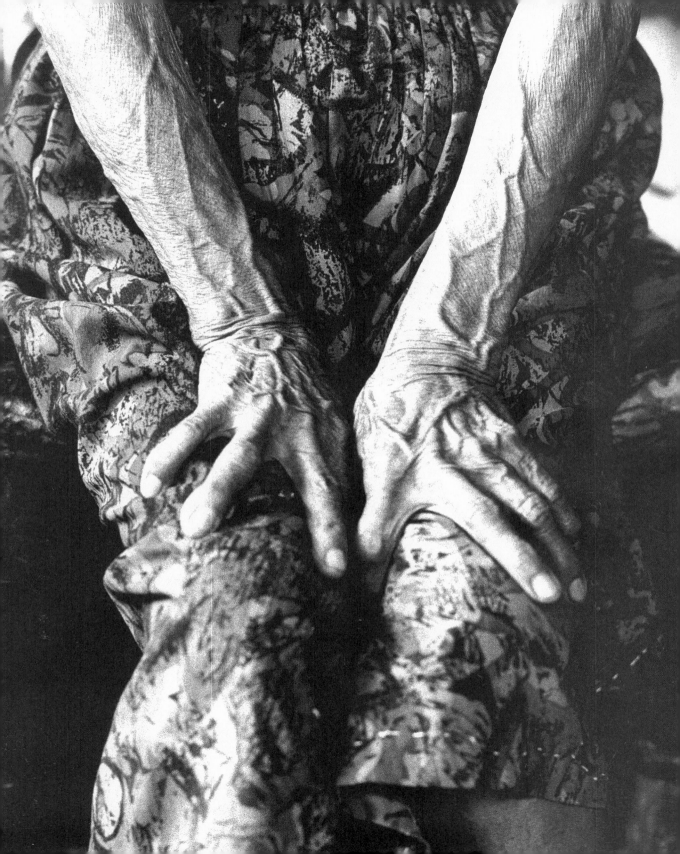

12

CONVERSATIONS WITH A BUTTERFLY

Shirani's pace was steady and quick. As we descended the steep hardened dirt road, he accelerated even more. These roads could turn into an impassable, gooey, sticky mess within minutes at the start of the area's frequent torrential downpours. I had to extend my usually long strides just to keep up. As the cadence of his footfall rebounded up from the rich soil in hollow rhythmic thuds, I lost step and began to fall back, already out of breath. I was no match in energy for Braulio's fifteen-year-old grandson. He was obviously leading me to the home of an eighty-five-year-old Brunca elder, Paulina Leiua, as rapidly as possible. He was taking his mission as guide and translator very seriously.

Glancing back over his shoulder and seeing my position, he slowed, allowing me to catch up. He was already at the bottom of the hill where the road circled back up through the cluster of houses on the valley floor. He pointed to a building and said, "That's the radio station up there on the hill. That's also where the only phone in the community is located."

Lost in a moment of reflection, thinking about the similarity of Leandis's difficulty in getting to a phone, I barely heard Shirani continue. "That's become the gathering place now. People line up to use it. Sometimes it's hours before a call can be placed. If it's busy at the other end, you lose your turn. People stand around and talk. Friends stop by to visit."

Welcoming the rest, I looked up at the little white building squatting beside the pencil-thin tower rising high above the church steeple that was next to it. "Competition," I aimlessly blurted out, my mouth in gear before my mind engaged.

"I knew somebody was coming to see me. Five days ago there was this h-u-g-e butterfly with eyes on its wings that came in. It came flying in, said some people are coming and then it left."

With his eyes falling, tracing the slope downward, Shirani's expression dropped. I tracked his gaze as he informed me, "Those there," and pointed to several square buildings across the street from where we were standing, "are the people's agriculture cooperative. That used to be the center of everything around here. Now it's only at harvest time."

His eyes darted back up for only a split second. Then, turning around on the heel of one shoe, he was again in motion. Leaving the road, he was now heading along a well-trod path leading down to a stream. The air cooled abruptly, and just beyond the ledge of the bank I could hear the gurgling of the water rushing in miniature rapids over large, rounded, cannonball-like stones. Inviting us to cross over, a narrow, precarious swinging foot bridge stretched out before us.

Shirani did not hesitate. He was on the bridge without a thought. Swaying and bouncing, he laughed. Taking one hand off the steel cable, he gestured for me to follow. I stepped on, immediately catching the swell of old boards creaking in a surge of waves brought on by his weight cavorting with wood and metal. He was on a high, and I was paying for it.

As he jumped off at the other end, I was riding a roller coaster. Gravity was attempting to collect his debt from me, trying to suck me over the side and into the ravine I was now directly over.

Being pushed forward on the crest of each new heave, I reached the middle of the aging apparatus. Instead of putting up a struggle, I became more fluid and gained my balance. With one foot on the single good board nailed on top of the older planks, my other foot flew through the air to catch the next peak as I "rode" the ripples to the other side. For a minute or two, after touching down, the ground seemed to be floating under me.

"Just a little farther," Shirani said encouragingly, as we began a slow climb. The avenue was hardly wide enough for two people on foot to pass. We cut through a neighborhood with small houses built high above the passageway on one side and down below on the shoal of the stream on the other. Reaching the summit of the rolling terrain, Paulina's homestead came into view. There was no

SHADOWCATCHERS

front yard. The steps up to the porch of her simple dwelling extended out to the very edge of the trail, seemingly welcoming a visit from any and all travelers.

Shirani, still on the path but standing at the open door, called out. There was no answer, although both of us could hear someone inside. He raised the pitch of his voice and cried out again. We waited. The sounds of movement inside continued uninterrupted.

Next, he tried knocking, his knuckles landing solidly but emitting little but dull raps. No one took notice.

Frustrated, he eased up onto the enclosed porch lined with doors opening directly into bedrooms and yelled a polite greeting, calling Paulina's full name. Again he paused in anticipation of someone acknowledging his presence.

In time, Paulina shuffled to an opening at the far end of the porch. Standing at the bottom of several steps, only her head appeared, just above the floor line. She seemed even shorter than her four-and-a-half-foot height.

"You've got to let me know you're here," she fussed, making up for any misconceptions brought on by her frame. "You know I can't hear. I'm always home. You've got to make yourself heard, I can't hear you. What do you want? Besides, who are you looking for and who are you?"

Paulina was disturbed as she came up squinting from her dark, earthen-floored kitchen. Shirani was embarrassed as he politely tried to find the words to explain. Getting right in his face as she stared hard from her lower vantage point, she was soon slapping her hands on her thighs. On understanding who we were, her initial scorn turned into chuckles of acknowledgment as she pointed out the chairs and took the first one she came to.

"I knew somebody was coming to see me. Five days ago there was this h-u-g-e butterfly with eyes on its wings that came in. It came flying in, said some people are coming and then it left. I told myself, 'Well, maybe some people are coming to see me.' And it was true, you came."

Giggling and clapping her petite hands on her legs, she looked at each of us through dancing eyes. Before she could continue, a large rooster walked into the house, up the couple of steps from where Paulina had emerged just minutes before, jumped across a pile of lumber stacked in the unfinished room, and, with a wild flutter, flew out the window. She spied it with keen interest. I wondered if the rooster had come in to talk to her, seen us, became frightened, and flew out. Then, she went on, "Like my people of long time ago, I follow the indications of the animals."

127

CONVERSATIONS WITH
A BUTTERFLY

Paulina's Story

Long time ago there was only the forest. We would go into the woods and get frogs, worms, and fungus to eat. The old men would have to make a fire with two rocks. Then we tied the worms up in leaves and fried them over our fire. After being baptized our diet changed to rice and beans.

We didn't use blankets. Long time ago there were huge trees and we would take the fiber inside the bark and mix it with leaves to make our bed. We used the bark for blankets. Back then we didn't wear clothes either. We were naked. I think it was better in those days.

We didn't know there was a God like there is today. The elders had all the power within themselves. They even had the knowledge to cure our illnesses.

There was the big chief who had more power than anyone else. Everyone thought of this person as a miracle. Not only was he powerful enough to cure illnesses, he had the special sacred prayers that gave him the power to see into the future. People feared him, and others who came after him, because what he saw came true. The people with that sacred power are gone now—they died.

The Woman Who Cried

There was this woman who lived in the mountains. Every day she would go down to the river in the valley to cry for her baby that died. She wept because the priests had told her that neither she nor her baby would go to the Creator, to God, because they had not been baptized.

God heard her cries and spoke to her people. He said to them, "You do not have to be baptized. You are immortal. You will never die."

To this day, those people still live up in the mountains. They never died, and they weren't baptized.

The Bruncas

A long time ago the Bruncas lived in a very quiet village without very many problems. It was the custom of the people in the old days to work together. The products were shared. The work was shared among all the

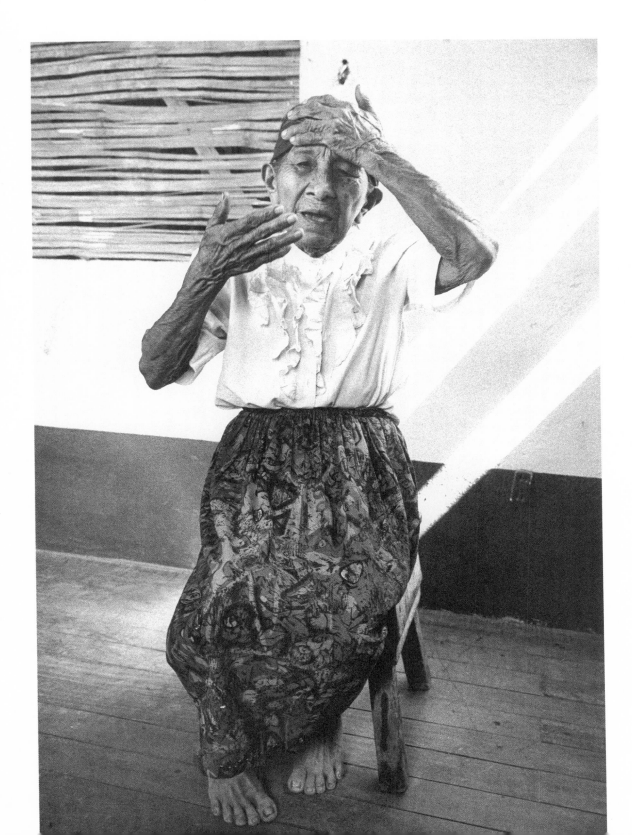

people and the product of that work was shared among all the people. We didn't need to buy things from other people because we had the things that we needed to survive. We had the essential products. Each person in the village received an equal share and could keep it or sell it. Each could do as he pleased with his portion.

When the white people came, they introduced money. Before that we had never used money. We had just traded products with others to get the goods we needed. So we started taking money for products, and some of the people sold all of their products and had nothing left for themselves. Many were disappointed, because they sold everything and had nothing to depend on to feed their families.

The new way of doing things seemed just like a trick to us, especially when outsiders saw our need and offered to give us more money. This time it was for our land and a lot of the people sold it, because we had no concept of buying and selling land. The land for was everyone. Before long people didn't even have land of their own to grow crops.

When we had the chief, he would guide us. There was no fighting for the land. It was all shared among the people. But when the chiefs died out, then the white people entered, invaded, and tried to command us.

Most of the land now has been taken by outsiders. They don't even let us take wood from off of it. Because we have so little land to live on, we tell ourselves that we are living like nigwas. A nigwa is a small perracid that lives on the smaller peaks. It's so small it doesn't need much land to live on.

We try to understand people. For the younger generation, it's difficult to show a kind spirit. Our youth work just for money. A long time ago they would work and work, even without receiving money. That kind spirit in the community has disappeared. There are only five elders who are still alive who haven't sold their land. They preserve it; not like the young generation that has sold it all.

Sharing in the Ceremonies

We used to have ceremonies. It was the time of the big drums and certain people would beat them to announce the beginning of the ceremony. Everyone in the village could hear them, and my grandmother would say, "Oh-h, get ready. They are calling us. We must go."

"There was one type of eagle that was called the Spirit Bird. Only a few people have ever seen it, and my grandmother was one of them."

Everyone would get excited and rush to the gathering to make prayers for the harvesting time. We would have a time of thanksgiving for the corn, rice, and beans. We would call on Baus, the name of the god, and pray only in our own language.

The Brujo and Baus

Baus was not God but a spirit who could send messages to God. God was represented by a snake. The witch doctor, a brujo, could send messages to Baus, who then talked to God. It was Baus who gave a special power to the brujo to be the translator so that our messages could be sent to God.

The translator knew when a snake was going to bite somebody. He knew when someone was going to drown or to die. He knew all these things. He could see into the future.

What I am saying is that Baus was a spirit and the brujo was a human. There was great respect for this translator, because he could tell when it was going to be a good harvest or a a bad one. The most frightening thing about him was that he had the power to make someone disappear, as well as transform them into something else.

The Singings of the Birds

A long time ago elders were finding their visions. Everyone had respect for the strange visions they saw. They used to tell about the ugly people, like monsters, but now there are no more of those.

The people, also, believed in the singings of the birds. We could understand the songs and the language of the birds. When one certain bird sang its song, everyone knew someone would be bitten by a snake and would die.

There is this hawk that will come along and say, "Kukaben, Kukaben," and the elders will say, "Oh, my god, my son or my daughter or one of my relatives is going to drown." And sure enough three days later after hearing this small hawk sing, one of their relatives was drowning. So it was true.

Now no one even believes in the singings of the birds or the visions of the old ones.

The Spirit Bird

There was a time when eagles appeared here and ate small kids. When they came close everyone in the village would run to the brujo to ask him make the eagle disappear, and he would do it. We were really afraid of the eagles, because once there was this big tree and two eagles came and had their nest there. Soon children began disappearing, and we all knew the eagles depended on children for food. They were being eaten by eagles. Yet, we respected the eagle.

There was one type of eagle that was called the Spirit Bird. Only a few people have ever seen it, and my grandmother was one of them. Now it's gone. It has disappeared. But we are still afraid that this bird will return, pick us up, and eat us in the sky.

It was left by God, but I don't know if God sent it or not. Only once in a while someone will see it. The elders aren't frightened by the thought of its returning. It is a very special thing for them to be able to see this Spirit Bird coming.

We are Bruncas. The elders of long ago said we came from the way of Colombia, so we think the Spirit Bird is a Condor. Before Colombia, we were told in the old stories, we came from Peru. My grandmothers told us that our great-grandmothers from Colombia brought these stories. So the relationship of this bird may have come from there. So, if that is true, it was the Spirit Bird that protected the people as they traveled here.

The great grandmothers, when they were speaking about this, said they heard that bird sing and followed its directions. My grandmother, when she was an old lady and I was a little girl in bed with her, would say, "Hear it! It's the Krus. It's here. It has come back."

I would take my blankets and put them over my head, because I was afraid of that great spiritual bird. So, I never heard it, my ears were covered.

13

THE BATTLE BETWEEN
THE SUKIAS

Ernesto looked at me through thick glasses. His weak eyes, magnified and over-filling the heavy frames, gave him an appearance of being in a constant state of happiness. Along with an expression tinged with a hint of mischief, his quick, big, toothy grin added to the sense of rapture he exuded.

For days, like clockwork, I had seen the eighty-seven-year-old elder begin each morning by dragging a bundled-up white sheet from the corner of his bright green house to his front yard. Meticulously he would untie the bundle and smooth the sheet out. Getting down on his hands and knees, he would reach out his long, thin arm and with hand extended level out the mountain of black and red coca beans. Painstakingly, he carefully made sure that no two pellets were on top of each other so that the sun would dry the entire batch evenly. He was taking his time with his crop that would bring in hard-earned cash.

During the day he would sit in the shade of his porch, like a centurion, keeping watch over his wards. In the late afternoon, just as the shadow of the roofline of his house would hit the edge of the huge square, he would rise from his chair and begin rewrapping the tiny orbs. Then he would drag the heavy load back into storage, his work finished until the following morning.

"Ernesto knows things," I had been told, "things nobody else knows anymore. You've got to meet him. You'll see."

Ernesto was grinning long before I got within talking distance. As I approached, he squinted hard. Part of his body was in the shadow and the glare

137

of the setting sun struck him full face. He said, "I was wondering when you were going to come to visit. I was told you were in our village, so I've been waiting. Hold on. Right now I have to take my beans up. Can't let the dampness get to them. They'll ruin. Then," he joked, "I'll have no more beans."

As I watched, Ernesto worked quicker than usual. Still paying close attention to every minute detail, down to the way he tied the knots, he followed his routine to perfection. Briskly returning, he only nodded a welcome as he passed, and pushed open the door in a rush entering his house. Swiftly walking over the spotless, polished concrete floor of his living room, he grabbed a high-back chair and strained ever so slightly as he lifted it out onto the stoop. Placing it squarely in front of his own already in place, he sat down, leaving me without a doubt as to where I was to sit.

"I figured you were coming over this morning," he chided. "It's always good in the morning. Something about morning air. It's good. But, I guess something came up for you."

I was taken back. It was true. I had actually planned on visiting him that morning, but had changed my mind. My plan had been to postpone long enough that I could procrastinate out of the encounter all together—weary from the trip and already thinking about home.

Spirited as he was, a trait he had probably been known for all his life, Ernesto began talking. As I settled down to face him, we squared eye to eye. Riding in my mind just over his voice, I kept hearing the haunting words, "Be careful what you ask for." I wanted to know about spiritual things, but the more I heard, the more I knew I had to come to peace with what I believed.

The Sukias

I knew the sukias. They were the healers. Some could work spells. One came to the village daily, another came three times a week. Now, none of them come. I knew what they did. They would cure people. Also, if you wanted them to make miracles or ask for them to make spells, they could do it.

There was a time I didn't really believe in sukias. So I wanted to test them. I went to one of the sukias and said, "I want a load of wild pigs."

The sukia said, "All right. I'm going to get here in the morning and tell you what you have to do."

"I knew the sukias. They were the
healers. Some could work spells."

So I met the sukia early the next day and said I was ready for my instructions. He told me I would find the wild pigs in a certain place, but I was to kill only four of them. I got my rifle and went with my brother-in-law to the place the sukia had told me to go. When we got there, it was too quiet. There were no wild pigs. I thought I had been tricked.

I was just going to return home, when we heard what sounded like a huge wild pig. Then I saw it, it was a white, wild pig. Behind it there came a bunch of wild pigs. After we shot the first four, my brother-in-law tried to follow the others that were running away, but he couldn't. They just disappeared in the mountain. The wild pigs really had appeared, just as the sukia had predicted or arranged.

I learned they could do what they said, but their way of doing things are very secretive. They will go at night into the mountains alone with a certain type of chair, sit down, and start singing. Late in the night they will return home and rest.

I once heard the sukias' songs. I couldn't tell what they meant because they were in a special language, a very old language, but I heard the singing in the mountains.

Sukias were dangerous people. You went to them to get them to do things for you, but you would have to pay them. If you wanted to do something to someone else, like make a person disappear and not ever return, the Sukia could do that, too. If you went to a sukia with a question, he would say, "Well, I'll tell you tomorrow."

The next day the sukia would have the answer. He would always be right, even if he did not know the people the question was about.

The Priest Versus the Sukias

The priests would never say anything to the sukias, but they would tell everybody not to believe in them. In spite of what the priests said, we knew the sukias had power. The priests were only trying to separate the people from the sukias.

There are still sukias, and they still help those who need their help.

Apprenticeship for Sukias

When sukias wanted to bring an apprentice into their society, they would take the person to their meeting. They would form a circle and talk among themselves about it. Each sukia would have a rock in his hand. The rocks were not like the crystals that priests used, instead theirs were the small rocks of adda.

When congregated in the circle, the chief would seat himself in the center and each of the others around the circle would have a small basket of little rocks and other secret things. Then, the chief would start the sacred teachings.

Then, when the person graduated, the chief would give him his own rock. He would then have his total power and would be respected by the people. That rock was the symbol of his power.

One of my friends in Punta Eranas had some of the sacred rocks. He got them from Indian cemeteries. He was once in a car and the car crashed. All the people in the car were injured except for him. He believed he didn't get hurt because of the rocks. I don't know if the power came from the rocks or it was from God. No matter, for me, I didn't want them because I don't want anything that comes from a cemetery.

Healing by a Sukia

I went to a sukia meeting once. I had a problem in my body near my stomach. It was all inflamed. When I got there, the sukia put me on a hammock. Then he sat close to me, and he prepared a special dish filled with very hot water. He took his rock and put it in the middle of the dish. Instantly I could feel the heat, my body became hot. After two or three minutes we were all sweating. Then, we took our clothes off.

Next he brought out teeth of an animal. I don't remember what kind of animal. He put the teeth very close to my temple, and it felt like he inserted them. I saw black blood coming from my cheeks, and soon I was covered all over with the liquid. Again, at my other temple he did the same thing. Then, he did it three times where I had the inflamation.

Next he took the peelings of the black plantain, held them over his fire and then passed them over my body. Once I felt the heat of the plantain peeling, I didn't feel any more pain. The bleeding stopped and my problem disappeared.

I made it home fast, because I was feeling good. Although it had taken me three days on horseback to get to his place, I got back home in about two hours. I traveled quickly.

I have had no more problems from that from that day to this, and I am eighty-seven years old. I am feeling sad, however, because I can see myself getting older and older. I have to be happy, however, because I have lived for a long time.

I will say to anyone who comes and asks me, "What's the secret of being so happy?" I will just answer and say, "Just take it easy with things that God sends. Accept what comes next with much thanks." And I accept it.

The Song of the Sukias

I have seen how hard the sukias work. They go out into the night and sing and sing, sometimes repeating their songs over and over. Sometimes they start to shout, like they are calling. Sometimes it sounds like there are many people singing in one place, but when you look closely it is one person alone that is singing and shouting. They are calling the spirits.

When they finish, it's as if they have been in a trance and they wake up. Immediately they say two things I can't repeat, then they stand, and shout. After that, they rest.

They sing loud and long to call the spirit, because the singing is a message to them. In turn, they listen to the spirits for instructions on what medicine to use for healing.

The Sukias Walk with the Spirits

The sukias walk with the spirits. The people are scared of them because of that. The majority of the population here has respect for them and are afraid of them because they are with the spirit.

Pita's Rock

There is another story about a sukia named Pita. Pita went to a meeting of invited sukias as a student. There was a lot of drinking, and he got drunk. While he was drunk, someone took one of his special rocks from him.

When Pita woke up, he was very angry. Then he recognized the person that had stolen the rock. He knew it was one of the wives of Telisforo, another sukia. She had seen him let his rocks slip and had been unable to resist taking one of them. When he recovered, he became so angry when he saw her, he went into a rage and killed her to get his rock back.

When Telisforo learned of this, he decided to disappear because his own life was in danger. He knew Pita would have killed him too.

Then, through a special ritual, Pita took some of Telisforo's power. Still Telisforo can cure some diseases and illnesses, but hasn't got the same power as he used to have during his best days as a sukia.

The rocks are very important. Without them, there is a loss of the healer's special power. Although the rocks are the most important objects of the sukias, they use other things as well. For different miracles they have skins of different animals. They have skins of wild pigs, small reindeer, and anteaters. When you have an illness, they will hit you all over your body with the skins. Different illnesses require different skins.

14

TALKS WITH SPIRITS

Chickens fluttered, cackled, and scrambled in four directions at once, as I entered Telisforo's homestead in the Talamanca mountains. Only a walking path led up the steep embankment to the old healer's house.

Built high on a mound, out of sight of any journeyers passing by far below, the aging structure seemed to be coming apart at the seams. Section upon section had been added as his family had grown. Having married once, then a second and third time, and finally a fourth time, Telisforo had followed the common marriage practice of the Bribri Awapa, a very secretive society of healers recognized by the people as spiritually anointed at birth by the Creator. Since he was an Usekra, or high priest, the most venerated among the sukias, no one questioned his decisions. Word of his powers to heal, his communications with the Mystery, and his ability to walk among the spirits had spread far beyond the land of the Bribri and across borders into other Indian territories. So many were the stories of Telisforo, I knew I had to meet him. Then, seemingly by chance, I met his daughter, Doris. Excitedly, I expressed my enthusiastic interest in talking with the great sukia. She readily agreed in leading me to him.

Finally reaching the level ground of the compound, I stayed close on the heels of Telisforo's daughter, who was leading the way. Doris called out. A hog snorted in disgust at our unwelcome intrusion from its burrow under the shade of a huge sheltering tree. Numerous pairs of human eyes quickly appeared from behind the dark confines of gaping cracks in the plank house's weather-beaten door.

She called again. Still, no one stirred within the shadowy sanctuary of the house; the peering dark eyes were unmoved. Doris hesitated, appearing puzzled. Then, throwing a reassuring glance in my direction, she repositioned her infant daughter, who was slung heavily over one hip, and walked with weighted steps toward the front door. She called out, this time much louder. A deep murmur, almost a surprised groan as of someone being pulled from a deep sleep, met her greeting and echoed back like muffled, rolling thunder.

I looked at the sky in search of the sound, which I thought to be an approaching storm, but the darkening clouds were still far across the valley on another mountain range. She smiled, knowingly. Straining from the burden of her human load, Doris motioned me up the steep makeshift steps of unhewn granitelike slabs leading to the porch. Still there was no one to be seen. Thinking the rumbling must, therefore, have come from behind the time-battered front door, I began carefully scaling the vertical rock incline.

As I scrambled up the last ledge to reach the creaky, sloping verandah, I kept my gaze fixed on the slatted door in anticipation of it abruptly opening. Suddenly I caught a slight movement out of the corner of my eye. Startled, I jerked around, half embarrassed, to see a dark, heavyset figure pulling himself with great difficulty upright out of a well-used, homemade hammock where he had been sleeping.

Telisforo stared at me, and right through me, with only one eye opened. As I stood speechless, waiting for Doris, his focus wandered as if trying to find me. His expression changed, the lines on his face instantly rearranged, from expectation to a questioning concern. With his head thrown back, as if listening, his only eye darted to pinpoint each new sound.

Telisforo's voice rumbled. Doris arrived breathlessly at my side and responded, rescuing me. Bribri words were exchanged. Telisforo relaxed and welcomed me, no longer showing any trepidation.

Kneeling down beside him I introduced myself. The porch being so narrow and not long enough for more chairs, I had no choice.

Clutching his tall, worn staff and rocking back and forth in his hammock, he grunted. I started to say more, he grunted louder. I stopped, believing him to be giving me a polite hint that he wanted to speak. Apparently satisfied that he was free to take his turn, he said, "I know you. I don't need eyes like you are using to know. I know why you're here. I can see the spirit, talk with the spirit. The spirit talks. It always tells the truth, no lies."

You have to work to cure, but you have to always work with God.
Nobody has worked medicine without God.

Swinging again, his gnarled toes walking the suspended seat forward and gliding just above the rough wooden slats of the floor as he swayed backward, he looked straight at me. I was taken by the intensity of his stare, although I knew his physical eyes were not seeing me. Yet, he was locked on.

Then, he turned his head skyward. For a moment he said nothing, then he continued, "No lies, only truth at that level. Yes, I know you. We can talk."

Telisforo Speaks

I still practice medicine, and it will never die until I'm gone. I was born with some knowledge, the rest I learned from the elders. It comes from two things, the ability of the individual and, also, the power of the Supreme Being. That makes me have the ability to practice medicine.

The elders watch the children. As soon as their abilities are recognized, they come to teach you what they know. They started teaching me when I was ten years old. Before that I was practicing alone without any teachings or teachers, but I already had an understanding. The child that is gifted starts at a very early age. Now I have actually been Jawa for about seventy years.

When I was twelve years old, I was taken to the region of Talamanca. San Jose Cabecar, the city there, is the center of studies for the Jawa. It's like the university of Jawa. Then I went to the riverside. I spent three years as an apprentice with the elders there. I learned by doing all the things they instructed me to do. You have to work to cure, but you have to always work with God. Nobody has worked medicine without God. It is a lie if someone tells you it works without God, the God of the Bribri.

All of the sicknesses of the world, I can cure. I haven't cured just one, I have cured many.

Sibu, the One God

In our belief we have only one God, not many gods. It's a lie that we have many. We have only one. Everybody comes up with his own idea of God and how they represent him. The name in Bribri of the one God is Sibu.

There is a similarity between one's language and God. Because there are many languages, there are many different ideas of God.

I've got to tell it the real way. To the witch doctors, the Jawa, there was only one Spirit left with the people to speak to them. That spirit is the one that speaks to us. The Spirit talks to other spirits. This spirit that talks with the witch doctors is like the messenger who talks with God.

There is life after death. When a person dies, the spirit lives on. This spirit of the dead person goes with Sibu. Kaska is the name of the place where spirits go. It is a place of paradise. All the people go there. I am going there.

Sibu said that when you die, you will go to be with him to this place. When Sibu passed by the earth, he left a message and a messager among all the people. That message came out through all the languages.

Spiritual Messages

There are people who can see into the future. I can see into the future. I can see what is going to happen to my people. If there is a big illness coming to my people, I will see it. Sibu is the only one who can see what is coming to my people and Sibu passes that information through the spirit messenger to me. When he knows what is going to happen, he will tell me. There may be variations in the message. Sometimes Sibu sends messages to the white people, sometimes to the indigenous people.

To receive this information, I have to concentrate in order to talk with the spirits. There is a stick that I use to make the bad spirits leave the body. All of the Jawa use one similiar to it. It's a special stick. We rarely use it, because we don't need it as much now. We use it only when the illness is incurable.

The Beginning

At first when this world was created, there was no light. Everything was dark. First there was just rock. Then, Sibu came along and he created earth so that the Indians would have a place to live.

The Bribri people were born in a place in Talamanca. We say that we were born, but we mean we were born like the seed of corn. God's thought was to produce us as a seed of corn. Afterward the seed of corn

broke open and the process of Indians growing as how we are now began. We were made into people, and we learned how to reproduce.

There was not a certain moment when God breathed life into the people. When Sibu created the seed of corn, he already had everything planned out. He knew that the seed was going to break open and that we were going to form into people. Nobody breathed any life into the indigenous people.

We are only sure of exactly how the Bribri people were born. Surely the whites and the blacks and the yellow, everybody else was made in a different form.

The Bribri were born at the same time and in the same place as the Bruncas, but they weren't born as a seed of corn. The Bruncas were born as a mountain pig. The Indian people left Amari with the mountain pigs and when they got to Boruca the mountain pigs became the Brunca people. They were taking these pigs to Boruca with the intent to kill them, but when they got to Boruca the pigs got lost. When the people came back the next day, they were people not pigs.

Supposedly after the pigs was a pack of monkeys. Those monkeys became the people that are now Teribes, the people from Teribe. The same thing happened. The people went away and came back the next day and the monkeys were people.

People like to tell these stories, but the reality is that all the indigenous people—the Bribris, the Bruncas—they all were born in the same place.

The Coming of the White People

There is only one God and we are all equal. The only thing that changed and is different is the many languages. Sibu allowed all the languages to exist.

A long time ago the Indians, the indigenous populations, were the only one on this continent. The whites came from a different place and have their own way of thinking. When the whites came here, they made the indigenous peoples adopt their way of thinking.

This land here used to only belong to the indigenous people and when the white people came here, they brought their own ideas, their own culture. Here in these lands, what we now call the Americas, there were no whites. We didn't know where they came from.

Some want the Indians to disappear, but that will never happen. Since I can see into the future, I will tell you I see a war coming. It will be for land. Many think the Indians will lose. Only Sibu knows the answer to that, but I know the fight will begin within the next ten years. The whites think they will probably win the fight. There is not a president who is willing to help the indigenous people. All of the indigenous people of the Americas will be fighting. At most the fight will be in about ten years, and a lot of lives will be lost. Because of what is coming, all the presidents and the leaders of all the countries of this continent need to be aware of what they are doing. It's principally important that they give this situation their full attention. It would help if it is recognized that we are part of the people too, and listen to what we have to say.

When people make war, God gets mad usually. When wars start God knows that people are going to destroy themselves. Everyone must realize that God does not create the wars. Then, because of the people who are making war, great sicknesses are created. God gets mad and allows that to happen, because people don't know how to care for each other and take care of the earth.

The sicknesses among the white people are because of all the wars they have started against people. Sometime those illnesses have come to the indigenous people, because there's a concentration of white people and the indigenous people have started getting involved with them. For that reason there's a lot of illnesses that we can't find medicines to cure because God has sent those illnesses down to us without a medicine. He did it as a punishment, but because we never had those diseases, we have no medicines for the cure.

Now there's almost no herbs left. All the trees and forest are being cut down for cultivation. Most of the herbs we used do not exist anymore. Finally, when all the sacred places are destroyed too, it's all over. We will have been destroyed.

The End of the World

The world will never end. That's an idea that was planted in the white man's head. The indigenous people believe that the world will continue. The only thing that will end will be the people. The world goes on and on and on.

The white people will eliminate themselves. The indigenous people will not end, they will just keep going on and on with the earth.

Live in Peace

My message to the Indian people is that they have to continue living in peace. Although God is very, very mad and he's allowing all the sicknesses, it's very important that we live in peace.

Telisforo stopped. In the silence, I waited in reverence for the profound words I thought would surely follow. As I stared down at the porch's smoothly worn planks, his gnarled toes twitched just beyond where I had squatted by his side. Then, his feet, cracked like ancient dried out leather, shuffled.

He spoke, but this time his words were not translated, as he struggled out of the hammock. Doris said nothing as her father, with hands walking before him in darkness, felt his way over the narrow porch and through a side door. Deliberately making his way down several shaky steps and across the unlit, dirt-floor kitchen, he inched his now shadowy form toward the back wall and pushed open another door to the outside. There he paused, not wanting to take all the time necessary, which would mean keeping his guest waiting. He stood quietly letting his water fly into the wind.

"When people make war, God gets mad usually. When wars start God knows that people are going to destroy themselves. Everyone must realize that God does not create the wars."

When he returned, he took the long staff in his hands. With his eyes glaring, seeing far beyond the black world of his blindness, he pounded fiercely on the wooden porch boards. The entire house shook. He swayed back and forth on his swinging cloth seat. The ropes supporting him strained, the rafters groaned under his weight. He was livid as he revealed how he could force disease out of the ground. Then he explained how the home of disease was deep in the earth, that was where it was born and took root. It hides in the earth, he explained, and Awapa, equipped with special sticks, would beat the ground to release the spirits so that the illnesses would not attack people.

"When people come for help, for a cure to their diseases, I go into the mountains. For three days and three nights I listen for the messages on how to heal the illness. During this time, I cannot sleep. I have to sing the sacred songs to go to Sibu. The songs are guarded because of fear they will be misused by those who do not know their power. Once I reach the Supreme Leader, I ask, 'Please show me which herb I should gather and give to my patient.'"

I was deeply moved by what Telisforo was telling me, although I knew he was careful to share with me only what he wanted to. Even with that, my own shadows, those murky forms that had clung to me so fiercely for so long, began to lose some of their intensity. I realized I had lost sight of who I believed God

153

TALKS WITH SPIRITS

"My message to the Indian people is that they have to continue living in peace. Although God is very, very mad and he's allowing all the sicknesses, it's very important that we live in peace."

to be. Having been taught in Baptist churches since childhood, I had the image planted in my mind that God was a white bearded old judge who sat on a huge throne high up in some illusive heaven. There He counted the sins of individuals and carefully kept score to see who was worthy of His love. From what I now was hearing, my concept began to loosen a little of its grip, and I considered the possibility that God could be a force all around and in me.

I liked the fact that Telisforo seemed not to be in subjection to God, not controlled by Him, not even to be His slave. His God was whole, and he was a part of it. That was why he could treat the whole person, unlike Western medi-

cine, which treats only the symptoms of a disease. For him everything was connected, and his duty on the circle was to work with the spirit.

As we left, Telisforo stood by the unpainted banister and waved in our direction, his ears translating the sounds of our steps to his eyes. They followed slightly out of sync in an attempt to "observe" our movement. Then, returning to the way I had found him, he sat down in the hammock he so fondly treasured. Only the top of his head could now be seen, and it nodded slightly. I could just see him swaying gently, as he had done during our conversation. His head quickly disappeared, however. I knew he had curled back up into his cloth cocoon.

15

THE MOUNTAIN OF DEATH

I had been to the mountain, a spiritual pinnacle, with Usekar Telisforo. We had talked about otherworld matters, about God and the Creation, about disease and healing, about the "forces," about positives and negatives. He had forcefully reminded me that there were natural laws. They could not be avoided, because the spiritual and the physical were one.

I was on a high as I reluctantly bade him farewell and stumbled along the soft footpath that dropped over a steep clay bank before reaching the dirt road where the car was parked. I knew that I would have to come down, but I was "on the wind," I thought. It is a marvelous thing to be "on the wind," but the wind is, also, a dangerous thing. It is a force, and it can kill. Still, it is a wonderful phenomenon. What I did not know was that I would have to face the balances that very day.

As Don slowly inched the car along the treacherous country road, maneuvering as best he could around huge rocks, I walked alongside to make sure he didn't straddle any. Puncturing an oil pan between Salitre and Buenos Aires would have stranded us for hours, if not days.

I replayed my visit with the blind elder of Talamanca over and over. The heat and the billowing dust didn't faze me. Only one thing nagged at me, and I fought it back until I couldn't any longer.

With my task as rock mover over, I got back in the car. I pointed out that the sun was speeding toward the horizon, and one thing was for sure: we would have to cross Cerro de la Muerte, the Mountain of Death. There was no way around the 9,000-foot peak.

ASUNCION
CERRO DE LA MUERTE
ALTURA
3335 METROS
INSTITUTO COSTARRICENSE DE TURISMO

Daredevil jockeys at the wheels of lethal freight-laden semis and self-appointed gods at the helms of buses loaded with captive victims raced to see which could pass the other on the next curve—the thicker the fog, the better the contest.

I became adamant. If, by the time we reached San Isidro, the last town before starting the ascent up the mountain, there was enough light left to safely get over the monster, we could go on. If it was dusk when we arrived, I was definitely getting a hotel room and spending the night. Don and Marcie, my translator, could stay or go on. My decision was firm. Fortunately everyone agreed, and the plan was set.

Now there was a race against time. I studied the map and checked my watch. Maybe, just maybe, we could do it. It would be close. Still, even under the pressure, Don's driving habits did not change. He was slow by local driving standards, and he stayed slow. In this situation his cautiousness was a virtue: he could not be intimidated by all the cars, trucks, and buses passing us. To his credit, he did do his share of passing, but only when there were no hazards.

It was late in the afternoon and the air had already started cooling when we finally hit San Isidro. The streets were alive with people, typical of towns in the area and for the time of day. Throwing caution to the wind, without even a debate, we continued on. It seemed the right thing to do.

No sooner had we gone through the last traffic light on the high side of town, than we started climbing. Everyone, however, seemed to be going in the opposite direction. Hordes of people, freshly bathed after the hard work of the day and dressed in their best clothes, were heading down the mountain, making for town. Some riding bicycles, most walking, each human cluster seemed to be in a rush to begin an evening of entertainment. Maybe they were fleeing what we were about to encounter.

As we rounded a sharp curve jutting out over a rock outcropping, I looked back to see the city spreading out on the valley floor and already falling far below. At about this same place there was a decaying concrete statue of Jesus towering on a cliff above us with outstretched arms and cupped hands—a vain symbol

159

THE MOUNTAIN
OF DEATH

embracing the masses. It would be my last view. The mountain was already squeezing us to her bosom.

The show was spectacular. Clouds rose from the valley floor, colliding with the monstrous mass. Pushed upward by the gentler lower breezes, the dense vapors caught the high winds in a mad dash over the peak. Immediate and near total darkness blew in with the fogs. At the places of the shadows' crossing the roadway, a wet trace of its passing remained to register its vicious trail.

In its ancient natural-world rhythm, rain fell in blinding horizontal bursts, diminishing to fine blowing mists before clearing. Then the ritual was repeated: the clouds again, rain, mists, clearing.

I was in the middle of the unfolding drama of nature. Call it the ceremony of the Grandfathers, a fundamental reference by American Indians to the dance of the venerated forces of creation. With visibility at near zero and with the headlights blaring back at near blinding intensity, I felt more like a victim of the ritual. I was not a willing participant.

I was seized by a deep, dark terror. Telisforo and I had talked of death, now I was on the Mountain of Death. And it loomed like a conqueror, taunting me. My worst fears resurfaced, growing more prominent with each curve. On one side of the precarious two-lane blacktop, cliffs rose hundreds of feet straight up. On the other side, cliffs dropped off a thousand feet or more. Round a turn and the cliffs would have switched sides.

Potholes, some a foot or more deep and yards wide, pitted the road. Dodging them was an exercise in futility. Broken pavement was common. In places the road was gone altogether, washed completely off the side of the mountain with chunks of asphalt strewn in long streaks all the way down the hillsides.

Although I was not driving, I was nevertheless clutching my own invisible steering wheel and negotiating each obstacle. My legs ached from riding nonexistent brakes. The palms of my hands perspired, and my body grew clammy. My eyes burned from strain.

Contending with the hazards of the venomous asphalt serpent was no game. Still there were other, more pressing perils. Daredevil jockeys at the wheels of lethal freight-laden semis and self-appointed gods at the helms of buses loaded with captive victims raced to see which could pass the other on the next curve—the thicker the fog, the better the contest. Oncoming or slower moving vehicles would, at times, be literally forced off the road to make way for the beasts. Some

lost, they couldn't get out of the way in time. Imprisoned in the bondage of the white night, they never knew what hit them.

Death roamed the mountain. White crosses erected by surviving family members or friends in every curve of the twisting bloodstained road testified to the power of the dark spirit. Sometimes one solitary concrete cross would stand starkly against the dark green foliage. Other times two and three would be grouped together in leaning bunches. I could almost feel the spirits, still earthbound, wandering the darkness, lost in the torrential downpours. They would be trying to find their heads or severed limbs, or a mother, a daughter, son, father. Dead? No, just trying to get home.

Earlier I had attended the Feast of the Little Evils, now I felt I was in the throes of the Night of the Devil on a road from or to hell. I refused to ask which.

I felt like I was still talking to Telisforo. There was a silent communication going on. I remembered his talking of the levels of awareness. For each level heavenward, there was a corresponding level down—positives and negatives. Rise a level, fall a level. For the serious student, comprehending that there was never one without the other was the Road to Wisdom. I had been to the summit

I had been to the summit
with the elder; now I was
being thrown into
the depths of the pit.

with the elder; now I was being thrown into the depths of the pit. Slowly it dawned on me that I was simply encountering opposites. I was learning that education can be a mean taskmaster.

Don tried to lighten my spirits. Jokingly he laughed, attempting to cut through the weight of the tension, "We could all die tonight. Here on the Mountain of Death. The headlines would be 'They Died on the Mountain of Death.'"

I furiously stormed back, "Stop it. Words have power."

"I was only kidding."

"I don't care. Words have power. You could make it happen."

Retorting, he vainly attempted to calm me, "I was only joking. Lighten up. Don't take things so seriously."

"I mean it! Stop it! Stop it now!"

The depressing atmosphere in the car could have been cut with a knife. As each one of us sulked, the quiet grew louder. My apology for my outburst did not help.

Suddenly I felt an impending danger. I broke the silence and murmured something about blowing a tire. Then, without warning Don swerved, missing the pothole, but the front wheel flew off the pavement. He fought to maintain control, pulling the car out of the washout and back onto the surface. The back tire quickly followed the front; it too had dropped into the ditch.

I was shaken, but thought it was over. It wasn't. The car was shimmying, then knocking. It was hard to stay on the road. We looked at each other. We knew, or at least we thought, a tire had blown. With no place to go—a hill straight up one side, a mountain straight down the other—we stopped in the road. Quickly we jumped out to inspect the damage.

We got to the back tire first. It was the one blown. Just to make sure everything else was okay, I ran, shivering, my teeth already chattering, to the front. Through the cold mist, water clouding his eyes, Don could see my grimace. He knew. The front tire was gone too.

We stood motionless, paralyzed, just looking at the disaster. For one brief moment, I became amused. It seemed with our staring we were watching to see if the tires would somehow miraculously fix themselves. Then the gravity of the situation began to sink in. We had a spare and a jack, but that was good for only one tire. That left one still flat and on the ground. There was no place to walk to for help. The nearest business was miles away, and even if we reached it that would not guarantee there would be a phone. Service stations were almost nonexistent. We were stranded in the road, on the outside of a sharp curve, halfway between nowhere.

Cars, trucks, and buses recklessly whizzed by, barely applying brakes even after seeing the car. At times the narrow two-lane suddenly became an impossible three as drivers murderously demanded the right of way, yielding to no one.

The bone-chilling wet quickly eroded the warmth I had enjoyed in the security of the car. There was no reclaiming it, sitting in the car for even a minute could be a death certificate. It was a "hit me" sign for any vehicle rounding the turn too fast.

When a young family stopped to see if they could help, my teeth were clapping so hard and my body shaking so furiously I couldn't talk. Only gibberish squeaked out. Fortunately my translator was able to communicate. The young man of twenty-something wanted to take his spare and put it on our car just to get us to a station. Drenched, we all worked to remove the wheel in hopes that his plan would work. It wouldn't, and his car was so packed that he had no room even to take one of us down the mountain. We waved, depressed, as he pulled off.

As his taillights faded into the fog, another family in a truck stopped. They would take one of us and the tires to the next station, but there was no room in the cab. The ride would have to be in the back of the truck.

We quickly agreed, we were desperate. I was elected to go and my elation came to an abrupt halt. Me, I thought, down this mountain, in the back of a truck! I enthusiastically agreed, faking it. Marcie volunteered to accompany me and fulfill her duties as translator. I was only mildly comforted, my dread taking priority with my emotions.

Marcie and I climbed in; Don threw up the punctured tire and held the wildly flapping tarp. In the sheer darkness we stumbled our way over the truck's cargo to the front of the bed. Surrounding us was a kitchen table, three stools, a cot, and a case of empty Coca-Cola bottles.

No sooner had I found a spot to crouch than the rig jerked, then lurched. Marcie grabbed my arm, and we both lost our balance and slammed together into the wooden slats of the supporting rails. Shaken, I regained a footing, only to be thrown back into Marcie as the driver slapped the gear into first and popped the clutch. We were moving.

Through the fluttering canvas, I saw Don standing in the rain by the car. He had already donned his poncho and a special waterproofed Australian-style hat he

In the break, lasting only for a split second, a lone star shined through. It radiated with a luster as if polished with a celestial wax.

had bought in Charlotte before we left. I could barely see his face, momentarily highlighted by the truck's oversized red taillights. His ghastly expression lingered, permanently etched in my mind, as we rolled away. I waved, but he couldn't see me. Still I waved long after he dropped completely out of sight. I had a horrible sensation that I would never see him again. I felt the loss as if it had already happened.

Marcie grasped my shoulder in an attempt to steady herself. I jumped, jolted out of my sadness, then flew through the air to one side as the truck slid, taking a curve much too fast. We were flying.

Suddenly lights flooded the back of the truck, blinding us and spotlighting our huddled mass. The bus had appeared from nowhere and was now impatiently riding our bumper only feet away and blinking bright to dim and dim back to bright.

"I'm moving," I said. "I'm moving to the tailgate. If something happens, I don't want to be trapped."

As I was nervously explaining, I was moving and Marcie was moving with me. "Shit if I'll go sitting still when I go, oh God, I don't want to go, but I'll not be trapped. I'll be jumping—trying—doing something to try to save myself."

A headlight moved to one side. "He's passing, the idiot's passing," I shouted, "here in this curve. I just know he's going to pass."

Then the other light moved. The bus was in the left lane. He gunned it. Passengers looked down on us. The bus braked, the passengers bolted. Their eyes were now as big as saucers. I saw their terror. Those who were staring at us saw mine. The bus was now back behind us. The driver, only inches away, was leaning over the wheel. He was irritated, his hands were vices on the hard plastic of the steering wheel. I was looking at the grim reaper in person. If he went, he was hell-bent on taking a lot of people with him. He was not going to go alone.

He changed gears. I knew no matter what, he was going to do it this time. The glare of one light moved off of us, then the second. This time there was no hesitation. The sudden blast of his engine deafened us. In an instant he was beside us, the bus only inches away from the side of our truck. Then, he was gone. I finally caught my breath.

SHADOWCATCHERS

Not to be outdone, our driver, small and timid as he first appeared, accelerated. He was not about to be seen as cowardly. Now nothing would slow him down. He was going to catch up to that bus and give it some of its own medicine. In his attempt to overtake the speeding beast, Marcie and I were thrown from side to side, sometimes ending up on top of each other. We rolled up tighter into balls, hugging our knees and praying for dear life.

In the midst of trying to hang on while hitting ruts, sliding around washouts, and dodging landslides, I foolishly peeked at the snake of a road we were flying down. It seemed we were airborne. Yet, something high above caught my eye. There was a slight fracture in the fog. A clear sky, made sparkling blue from a brilliant full moon, glistened. In the break, lasting only for a slpit second, a lone star shined through. It radiated with a luster as if polished with a celestial wax. I continued, with the truck's bouncing and shuddering, to look in its direction long after the fogs returned and covered its glow.

From the beginning of our descent down the mountain, I had made up my mind that I was going to die. Then, when the star appeared, a peace came over me. I was going to be all right. I was all right. And with the peace, I thought I heard a voice I believed to say, "I will take care of you. I always have. I always will.

"There is only one existence. When you know that, you will understand."

I remembered that years earlier I had heard, but didn't take to heart, the words of an elder, "The Creator cannot separate himself from the Creation. It cannot be done. The Creator is a part of everyone, of everything. Rely on it."

I leaned my head over to Marcie, which was not far since we were hard pressed against each other, and said, "It's all right. We're not going to die. We're going to live."

I bowed my head into my knees again and said, "Thank you."

When I did the driver began crossing into the left lane without slowing. He was off the road now. I grabbed Marcie as a fear rose up into my throat. She was rigid. We were both bracing for the worst. Then, he hit the brakes hard. We tumbled toward the front, rolling into the empty Coke bottles. I knew it was over. So much for my short-lived peace of mind.

The truck came to a quick stop. There was no crash. I heard the door slam and the sound of feet on concrete. I jumped to look out. We were at the service station.

Hesitating only to thank our kind driver for giving us a lift, I hastily rolled the defective tire into the repair bay. The attendant wearily scratched his head

and checked his watch. It was late, almost quitting time. Alarmed that he might decide to close before he could fix the flat, I began pleading. Marcie listened, then quickly realized after my second breath that the attendant couldn't understand a word I was saying, and began translating into Spanish. She was a sentence behind and struggled to catch up. It didn't even dawn on me that I was incapable of communicating. When it did, I let her take over.

Stunned by my onslaught, the attendant stood motionless. When things settled, he said, "This is the tenth tire I've had to fix tonight. A little above average. I could fix them all night, if I stayed open."

With a condescending nod of his head and a patronizing smile, he added, "I'm sorry. I'm very sorry."

Taking the tire, rolling it to the changer, he adds, "I'll get on to this for you."

No sooner had the words come out of his mouth then a car slid to a stop by the gasoline pumps. The missionary was frantic. He, too, had hit a pothole, rupturing a tire and had to get on to San Isidro as soon as he could. He didn't want to be traveling the Mountain of Death after midnight, and the clock was ticking. With his shoulders thrown back, and in an authoritative tone, he made it clear that he thought his tire deserved prompt attention—even before mine.

Sauntering over to him, after surmising him to be a North American, I asked if he was from the United States. He was; my theory had been correct. The Bible on his dash and bundles of literature on his seat told me the rest.

He was not in a talkative mood, at least not to me. It was the attendant who drew his attention. He was not about to be distracted.

Knowing that he was going up the mountain, right by our disabled car, I asked if he would allow us to ride with him after our tire was fixed to get to our car.

"My jack is not working right," he became agitated.

What I wanted to say was, "That's a lie. How in the hell did you get the jack to work to get the tire off your car and your spare on!" But I bit my tongue and politely stammered, "We . . . we've got a jack, and it works. We won't need yours. If you could just drop us off where my associate is waiting . . ." My voice trailed off for a second. Hoping to work on his guilt, if he had any, I picked up the tempo and added, "in the cold rain."

He retorted, "I've got to get to San Isidro. It's late now. You know how dangerous this mountain is, especially at night. In the rain."

He went on, trying to convince me it was not in his best interest or mine, "I know how it is sometimes. I could get tied up . . . may take longer than you or I figured. Besides, you're coming down the mountain and you'll be on in Cartego, I'll still have to go over the top and, then, down to San Isidro. I'd better not chance losing any more time."

With a condescending nod of his head and a patronizing smile, he added, "I'm sorry. I'm very sorry."

I thought, You surely are.

All the while our exchange was going on, the attendant was listening, trying to translate some of the English in his head. Fretting with the tire, he got Marcie's attention. Cupping his oily hand, smeared with black grime from a long day's work, he motioned for her to come over. Using the excuse of pointing out the puncture, he spoke in Spanish, "I've been to the States. I've got a brother that lives in New Jersey. I understand. If you let me fix his flat first, then I'll close so no one else can come in. If you're not in too big a hurry, I shut this place down and I'll take you up the mountain and help you get it back on. That way we'll know that it's on and you can get on your way."

In a hurry, I thought, after Marcie whispered what he had said, how can we be in a hurry.

I told her to tell him, "Yes, we would be happy to wait." Then, I added, "Be sure to tell him, 'Thank you.'"

As the missionary wobbled his tire to his trunk, lifted it, and put it in, I asked, "Would you be kind enough to tell my friend that we are getting the tire fixed and will be back soon, not to give up. You can't miss the car, it's in the road right at a curve. Can't miss it."

He looked back and syrupily intoned, "I'll be glad to."

He was in his car and, with a click of the gears, he was gone.

I had my doubts that Don would ever get my message.

Crammed in the four-by-four pickup, heading up the mountain as fast and as recklessly as we had come down, I nervously mused, "At least I can see where I am going this time," as the attendant boasted that he knew every inch of the highway. He went on, "I know exactly the hole you hit. A lot of people hit it, too. Everyone knows that one. Your friend will be all right. Everyone who travels this road much watches out for it. So, they'll be a little slower coming round that curve. Won't hit him."

Then, he added a word of caution, "When you get past the station on your way back, watch out for the hole at Kilometer 27. That's the one that guy in a hurry hit. Been three tires blown from that one tonight."

When the reflection of our lights drew Don out of the shadows, I breathed a sigh of relief. I never thought I would see him alive again. Yet, there he was, floppy hat pulled down to his ears and teeth chattering so hard he could hardly talk. But he was safe, soaked and cold but safe, and so were we.

The Mountain of Death, hungry for victims, had been robbed of its prey this night.

16

GOD AND THE DEVIL ARE BROTHERS

Leading the way, Francisco disappeared into the dense banana grove. Having no path to follow, I dashed to stay close on his trail. As the huge leaves slapped me in the face they momentarily blocked my view, making it difficult for me to chase him. I caught only occasional glimpses of his plaid shirt flapping in the wind as he rounded one tree and flew out of sight behind another. At times only swaying branches informed me that he had passed and that I was still headed in the right direction. It was as if he had forgotten I was unfamiliar with his territory.

With dogs barking in the distance, and not wanting a confrontation with them without Francisco for protection, I sucked in more air and sprinted. Just as I threw myself into building speed, figuring I was in for a long hike, the grove ended. I was stunned, almost tripping over myself to break my mounting acceleration, as Francisco's compound opened before me. Had he not told me to follow, I would never have known anyone could have lived that close to the road and still be so completely hidden in the dense vegetation. Yet, I was deep into Guaymi territory. This was an Indian country divided in half by the Panamanian and Costa Rican borders, with the Guaymi separated from each other by a political boundary.

Embarrassed, I stumbled over the neat, cleanly swept courtyard trying to regain my balance and a degree of composure. I was relieved when Francisco paid no attention to my clownish movements and made directly for his wife and children. He warmly embraced them and, apparently, sought to calm their concerns about my intrusion. Only the day before during our meeting in the San

"Indian women used to have their children without any problems. They didn't need operations or anything like that. But now white men have come in and caused a lot of the women to doubt the curanderos..."

Jose home of a mutual Brunca friend, Jose Carlos Morales, he had studied me carefully as he sat silently listening to my request to talk to him about Guaymi spiritual beliefs.

Disinclined at first, he later hesitantly agreed after seeing that I had not come to study his people but to personally learn from them. It was obvious he had weighed my sincerity to be higher than that of an anthropologist, otherwise he would have flatly turned me down. Without phones in or near his home, however, he had no way of communicating his decision to his family. My presence, therefore, had surprised them, catching them completely off-guard.

After introducing me to his family, Francisco motioned me over to sit with him under the shade of the sloping roof extending out from his family's sleeping quarters. Looking around for a stool, I realized that what I took as a porch was a very useful open but covered dirt-floored room, which was used not only as a family room, but also for sewing and, with clothes hanging about, as a closet. At the far end a worn, sagging hammock hung from the rafters. Francisco claimed it immediately.

Swaying back and forth, a grunting hog and pecking chickens cavorting next to him, Francisco relaxed. With his legs draped over each side of the hammock, he began sharing his way of life as I listened to his words. Even his wife, working in the middle of the courtyard over an open fire in her kitchen without walls or roof, strained to catch his words.

The Rightful Role of Indian Doctors

Indian people want to maintain and preserve traditional medical practices. However, there are a lot of Western doctors who say that our doctors, the curanderos, are witch doctors, and that we are practicing bad medicine through superstition. These Western doctors are trying to extinguish our way of healing. They do not understand that some sicknesses are only with the indigenous people. These the curandero knows how to cure, because they were here long before Columbus arrived.

We are not ignorant. Our healers understand diseases they are familiar with, but the Spanish brought strange diseases with them from their world. Even to this day our curanderos have no basis of knowledge for treating them, but Western doctors do. So we welcome their help in areas where they are qualified.

We are beginning to believe we have to use both methods for treating illnesses, depending on what kind of sickness there might be. But if we cure ourselves, then we're not going to the doctors or buying medicine from them, and that threatens them.

Indian women used to have their children without any problems. They didn't need operations or anything like that. But now white men have come in and caused a lot of the women to doubt the curanderos, because these men have convinced them they are bad for using traditional medicine. So, instead of going to the curanderos and the sukias to have successful deliveries and healthy babies, they go to doctors in the cities.

The Sukias

We have two types of traditional healers. There are the curanderos and the sukias. The curanderos learn the properties of herbs and plants, whereas the sukias are born with an innate God-given ability to cure. They call on God directly through their sacred songs that only they can sing. Then, they receive a spiritual message on what to do to cure the person.

Still, the curanderos and sukias work together. There's not a conflict between them, it's a complementary thing because the primary interest for both is for the sick. The sukias, however, have more experience than the curanderos, because their knowledge comes from a spiritual source.

GOD AND THE DEVIL
ARE BROTHERS

There is some distinction in their roles, though. The sukias are teachers. They are our wise men. We recognize them as advisors, healers, and teachers. They work for the well-being of the community. In turn, everyone works to serve them. It is a big responsibility being in that position.

I have practiced some medicine. I know a little bit, not a lot . . . some. My grandfather was a curandero and a historian. I know some of what my grandfather taught me. I am not a sukia. However, it would be rare for a sukia to admit he was one.

The Spirits

Spirits are all around us. Some of them are angels that are the messengers sent by God to be with us, others are the spirits of the dead. God sends the bad spirits somewhere else on another path, but the good spirits he receives. Eventually they will be able to return, but it's after the people today are gone. It has to do with God putting new people on the earth.

There are good spirits in white people, too. When they come back, they'll come back and inhabit the place where they originated.

The Devil and God Are Brothers

The devil and God are brothers. They both can give power to humans. If God gives humans power, it is good. If the devil gives power, it's bad. Sometimes people will go between good and bad, because there is a curiosity with power.

Even though what the devil would do is bad, God still loves him because he is a brother. So when the Europeans came over here, Indians saw them as people who had been given power from the devil because they crossed the ocean against the instructions of God. The Indians realized that the Europeans had come to claim the land and destroy the people.

They came with the Bible, talking about God, but in their hearts they came with a different thought and belief. There was a conflict between their words and deeds. The Europeans saw our natural resources and the possibility of riches to be made from robbing them. That's all they were interested in, and that greed controlled them. They cared nothing for the people they encountered, so Indian people suffered from their abuse.

The Story of Creation

Long ago the world was very poorly treated and a young one was born named Navu. This was God.

The devil is the older brother of Navu, God, and the devil didn't want anyone else to share the world. He wanted to rule it alone.

Soon there was a fight between the older brother, the devil, and the younger brother, God. But the younger brother, he just kept growing and becoming stronger. He would play with his mother and hide from his older brother. Finally the day arrived when he had grown quite a bit and he turned himself in to either be killed or left alone.

At that time the moon and the stars and the sun were living here on this earth. It was long before my people came into existence here on this earth.

Then the devil and his family killed God. They killed God! Before dying, however, God told his family, "After I die, do not eat the food for four days because it will be contaminated by the devil. After the four days, you can eat because I will come back to life—resuscitated."

SHADOWCATCHERS

After he was dead, the devil took power and he declared, "From now on, I am the All Powerful. All the food I make, you will have to eat."

But God's family obeyed what he told them to do. When the time came for God to come back, a small plant of cocoa grew. Within three days it became big. On the sunrise of the fourth day, the day the family was supposed to eat, there was a chicken on top of the cocoa plant. It sang and crowed, as chickens do, until all the food had been laid that they were supposed to eat.

So the family was very happy, because they knew the crowing of the chicken was heralding the return of God. So God came back.

But the fight between Navu and the devil over who was going to rule the world was not over. So the competition grew. One day the devil challenged God to see who could make the most beautiful things. The devil said, "Whoever succeeds, all those things will belong to him."

God accepted the contest and won. Then God made a doll out of mud and he said to the devil, "You call it and if it comes to you, he's yours. If he comes to me he's mine."

So the devil began to call him, but he never came. The devil kept calling, but still it never came.

So God went to his mud doll and blew in his face, blew on his arms, and every part of his body, and he said, "Come with me." And the clay doll came running to him like a little child. And so now he was with God. It is for this reason we have dark skins, brown, the color of the mud from the land. God saw that the doll was able to live very well here, so he left him there.

Still, the fight continued between the devil and God.

God said that he was going to make trees, animals, birds, fish, and water and everything that the doll needed to live.

Again the devil said, "If You make something good, it is going to be yours, and if I make something good, it will belong to me."

So they started with the animals. They began making animals. The creations of the devil were very ugly, but those that God made were very pretty. So God won again.

Next they looked at the sea. God said, "If you can make the water salty, it's yours. If you can't, then I'll put salt into it and it'll be mine."

The devil said that he would be able to do it. The devil always began first. The devil began to put salt into the ocean, but it never became salty.

So God took just a little bit of salt and put it in. He said to the devil, "Taste it." He did, and it was very salty now.

"I did it, so now it is mine," God said.

Throughout the battle, God continued winning. So God said to the devil, "You can't compete with me, because I beat you in everything. I am stronger than you."

The sun, moon, and stars still lived on the earth. God spoke to them and said to the sun, "Light up the world so that the human being can live."

Then he said to the moon, "You have a duty, too. You are going to be for women."

Next, he told the stars, "Your lights are beautiful. You will sparkle in the skies for all to see."

Finally, he spoke to all of them at one time, "The sun is for men so that they can work all day and take care of their families and maintain them. The moon is for women and you will be responsible for directing the time of their menstruation." Then, he added, "Make sure you are faithful in carrying out your tasks."

To everyone, God warned that the devil was going to be living very close to earth, but he promised that the devil couldn't touch anything unless there was an order from him. Just for added protection, God put angels on the earth to watch over his creation and to be his messengers to let him know how everything was going.

So all the enemies of God became like servants to him. All the bad animals, the king of the serpents, were taken away and all the good ones were left to stay here with us.

A World for the Mud Man

Since God had put man on earth, he needed to provide for him. So he told the king of the serpents that he was going to be the guardian of the rain, the clouds, the air, and all the waters. All the bad animals had been gotten rid of, and the king of the serpents was now tame.

With the king of the serpents to stand guard, he made just a little tiny pool of water. At that pool of water, he was going to give a name to all the animals, as well as man, so that they could all live together.

God told all the animals to come to the tiny pool so that they could receive a name. He also called the doll that was made out of mud to come, although he was now a grown man. God called on one of his angels to come to the pool to give names to some of the animals, but not to others, so that the mud man would know which ones he could and couldn't eat.

So the little mud man was at the side of the pool and the animals came one by one. As they approached, they would say their names in all the different languages depending on where they came from. Upon saying his name each animal would drink from the pool. If he didn't have his name, there wasn't any water for him. And that's how they did it. Each animal went giving his name without being afraid at all. Birds also.

That was how God created everything on earth and that's why we're here together with the animals.

From this mud man God created one mother and one father and from them came different children. Each of these children spoke different languages and so God sent them to different parts of the world, because that's how he wanted it to be.

The Science of Animals

Many years ago the animals wanted to be more than friends with the Indians, they wanted to mate with them. The sukias and curanderos said no, they rejected this. They said, "You can't be friends with us, because you have one kind of blood and the humans have another and to mix that wouldn't be very good. God didn't want it that way."

The snakes and the serpents did the same thing. They wanted to join with human beings, too. The sukias said that relations between snakes and human beings were not good because God said it was not.

Human beings paid close attention to the animals and thought they were beautiful, however. So everyone began to study them, including observing the designs on their bodies. I call it the science of animals. The snakes are painted a certain way. Women copy patterns on their bags according to the patterns on the snakes. The hats I make are similar to certain patterns on animals. That's the science of animals.

Learning from the Elders

Thank God I always listened to my father and my grandfather. Now I remember their stories and recognize the significance of them. From the age of fifty to sixty years old a person begins to be recognized as an elder. That's just in years, because it takes more than age to be an elder. It takes wisdom, too. As I get older, I realize how wise they both were.

I am saddened that many of my people don't remember the stories anymore. Much of the reason for that is because many anthropologists come into our territory and record our stories. Then, they would say the stories didn't mean anything. So, the people, little by little, would not retell them. Soon the people began forgetting them until they didn't remember them anymore.

I remember. So I sit with my own family and I tell them the stories I heard when I was their age. Now that my grandfather has died, I feel I am helping to carrying on our culture.

Preserving the Land

The land and the mountains are very important to us. The whites are blindly deforesting land wherever they can. They're taking out all the plants and the animals. Fortunately, where the Guaymi live there's still forest, there are still animals, but lots of people come in and hunt without our permission.

We live off of our land. The mountains provide the food for our families and the building material for our homes, and that is being destroyed.

Before Columbus, we had about two hundred different kinds of food—potatoes and squash and corn, just all sorts of things that was our food. Then colonists brought all these strange foods from outside. We don't know how to take care of them because all sorts of chemicals are needed to take care of them. If we don't have the chemicals, which cost money, then we can't take care of the foods.

We still have some foods that are naturally resistant to disease and insects and don't need chemicals. We do not tell the people from outside what they are because first people wouldn't believe us, then they would come in to see for themselves. Also, they could bring their diseases and destroy the crops. We just don't tell anyone anything.

"It's time to live in harmony.
Everyone with everyone.
We know that we all are brothers."

Order of Life

In Guaymi belief, the trees are in first place. In the second place come the animals and the birds, and in third place are human beings. We were able to live on this earth because the trees gave fruit, that was something the humans could eat. So we're like in third place on earth. The fourth place is the white people that came in and started destroying everything.

We value nature. We're trying to conserve it but not to govern it. We try to live in harmony, because we know all of life is very important.

We Need Understanding

It's time to live in harmony. Everyone with everyone. We know that we all are brothers. It is very important to get a message out to the non-Indian people, because we feel like brothers with them. Hopefully we can achieve an understanding between both cultures in order for all of us to live well and have respect for each other. If we do, God will see that everyone is behaving well together.

This entire message I send to all the people of the entire world. I hope for harmony, peace, and unity between all peoples so that Navu, God, gives all of us better health and longer lives.

17

THE STAR MAN OF KUNAYALA

I was in a frenzy. Gritzko was late. It was already 4:30, and the Kuna-appointed interpreter was a half hour behind the timetable. He had strictly ordered that we follow the timetable in order to meet the 6 A.M. flight to San Blas. He had been downright adamant.

"The pilot won't wait for anyone," he had said the night before. "We have to be there ahead of schedule to make sure we get a seat. The plane fills up fast. First come, first served, even with tickets. It's always loaded, most of the time overbooked. Got to be there. Miss the flight, you miss it. Only one out a day, and that's at six."

Now he was nowhere to be seen. I paced. Groggy, still half asleep, I nervously counted the steps between the door and the balcony of my hotel room. Back and forth, over and over, I multiplied the steps from yards into feet. Every third crossing, I went out onto the balcony to see if his tattered brown Toyota had pulled up to the hotel's entrance. With each look, my agitation mounted.

"If I'm not there by 4:30, call me. Sometimes it's hard for me to get up early," he had warned.

More alert after my unwelcome predawn exercise, I picked up the phone and rang for the operator to place the call to Gritzko. There was no direct dialing; the hotel's telecommunication system had not been updated. Ring, ring, ring, one after another ring. Minutes passed and the ringing continued. There was no answer. It was early, too early for the operator to be on duty, and too early for me to be up as well.

Glad that there was no physical emergency, I was nevertheless upset. I had a plane to catch. I thought about taking off for the airport without him, going on to San Blas, but I stopped—God, he had the tickets.

Grabbing up my gear, I rushed out the door, pushed "down" for the elevator, and picked up my pacing as I impatiently waited for it to arrive. It was slow in coming, too slow for the time of morning. No one else was stirring and still it was slow. Finally the call light went off; I marched to the center of the door, eager to enter. Even the doors hesitated. Then at a snail's gait the doors crawled open. I hit 1, the doors creaked closed. I was moving—6, 5, 4, 3, I thought 2 would never come. Finally, 1 lit up. My nose was in the crack as the lobby inched into view in front of me. Squeezing my bags and my two-hundred-pound frame through, I was already moving toward the operator's station before the doors of the elevator had fully opened.

In a mad dash I crossed the foyer, hard hit by the eerie stillness greeting me. Around a corner an unanswered phone rang endlessly. The operator was nowhere to be seen, her booth was empty. I raced for a pay phone, dropped a coin, fumbled blurry-eyed for the number, and dialed.

There was no answer. I held on, listening to the irritating jingles. I waited, determined to wake him if he was still there, but hoping that I had missed him and he was on his way. As I started to hang up, moving the receiver away from my ear, I barely heard a soft, "Hola!"

"Gritzko!"

"Esteban?"

"What time is it?"

"It's 4:45, Gritzko," I excitedly demanded.

"I'm coming. I'm on my way. You up? Hard to get up. We'll make it," he hung up.

Questions about going to San Blas began to rise in my mind as I pushed through the lobby's front doors and joined the hotel's militarily attired armed guard, automatic rifle slung over his shoulder. He watched me, our eyes never meeting. The smells of tropical Panama City rushed my nostrils. The damp, dank scent of mold, having ridden in with the night, permeated the air. I breathed deeply, remembering.

I had been here before, many times before. In 1969, on my first trip as a journalist, I had come to Panama to cover an assignment on Aligandi, a Kuna island in the San Blas chain. For several years, year after year, I had returned to

Aligandi. On my last trip, in 1980, I had not only gone to Aligandi but to the Darien Gap as well. Now I was back and the shadows of my earlier trips danced around me in the dimly rising light. For one brief moment I was caught up in the experiences of that first visit.

I was in a time warp or déjà vu. I was back flying across the jungle, spotting the dot of an island crammed with roof-to-roof huts. I was landing on the narrow dirt strip, greeted by the Kuna women colorfully adorned with molas and gold rings that they wore through their noses.

I savored the moment, then it was gone. I was back in the present with the strange sensation I was home, or at least going home—back to the Kuna—only this time it was unlike previous visits. This time I had come with a different motive. Before, I was on assignment, although I had always been drawn to indigenous peoples. Now I had come seeking for personal reasons, spiritual reasons.

Yesterday, while meeting with the young Kuna representatives of the Asociacion de Kunas Unidos por Nabguana, I had met with the same emotional rush. As Marcial Arias, the association's determined president, talked, I listened intently as he told of the Kuna's origins.

"Know why the moon has black spots?" he asked, proceeding undauntedly without a pause.

"Our ancestors came at the same time as other animal groups. This was the time of the Neles, wise people with special powers. It is difficult to describe Neles. They're like shaman. There is no exact translation. These ancestors could make thunders come down with their eyes. If anyone was ill, the Nele could tell what was wrong just looking at the person. They were born with these powers. Could talk with all things in nature.

"That was the time of monkey men. From them came two people, a brother and a sister.

"The boy wanted to have sex, but he was not allowed to have sex with other animal groups. One night he touched the sexual organs of his sister.

"Next morning she knew someone had been touching her. So the sister said to herself, 'I'm going to use the parasites that live on the head, lice.'

"She prepared a special fruit, the kind that makes black ink. She left the fruit on the table and told the lice to wake her up when the person came to touch her.

"When her brother was caressing her body, he got this ink from her hammock. In time the ink got really black.

"Each day the boy went to the river to try and clean up. The girl had the power to dry up the rivers. So he couldn't get it off.

"Every morning the girl would prepare breakfast. One morning her brother didn't show up. He had fallen asleep by the river. She went looking for him and found him. She came by his side and talked to him.

"'What happened to you?'

"He said he had stomach problems and a headache—excuses. She became very worried, but she suspected the brother of being the one touching her. Then, she saw black stains on the hammock. He left. He left his tools and went into the mountains. The girl kept calling him not to leave.

"'Why were you not sincere? If you had asked me, we could have worked it out,' she said.

"But the brother didn't listen. He just kept walking away. Today he is the moon and that's why the moon has black spots."

Marcial continued, "We are carriers of the spirit. Many things our people have to have in our minds, like rites for the dead, our history and our legends.

"Elders today are asking the people to learn. When an elder is ready to die, he wants to have someone to learn, but it is hard to find anyone willing to receive this knowledge. Ten years of study are required to become knowledgeable to do medicine, to sing the song for dead people.

"Every day the elders sing. They pray to stimulate the Kuna to work the land. Every song is to defend the motherland. The land is our pharmacy, our house, our grocery store. That is why green areas must remain. Destroy the tree, the earth will die, humans will die."

My enthusiasm for returning to San Blas had grown while Marcial talked. When he had finished, I asked him which island in San Blas would I be flying to. He immediately corrected me.

"San Blas is the former name. Our territory is now called Kunayala, Land of the Kuna. You will be going to what used to be called San Ignacio Tupile. It is now Dad Nakue Dubpir. The elder there is Carlos Lopez, Inakelinya. He's eighty and his title is Cacique General Kuna since July 1992. He's one of the three elders who preside over all Kuna affairs."

Unconsciously, having been caught up in recollections, I had started rhythmically patting my foot loudly on the concrete steps of the hotel. In annoyance, the para-

military guard cast a sour expression without acknowledging my presence while walking as far as he could to the opposite end of the entrance.

I heard Gritzko's car before he arrived. Turning, I saw him round the corner in a flurry. He was already talking before I was in the car. I caught the last part of his sentence, "but we'll make it."

Winding around the deserted streets of the city, I became confused. "I thought we were going to the airport. Where are we going?"

"I just told you. We have to get a cab. I have to drop my car off at my apartment. Taking a cab from there. You don't think I'm going to leave my car in the parking lot, do you? Somebody'll rip it off."

I looked at the car, started to respond, then thought better. At least we were on our way. Maybe we would make it, but I wasn't so sure. We had only fifteen minutes before flight time.

We went with all the speed his car could muster. As we turned from one street onto another, then down a narrow lane and back onto a wider street, the character of the neighborhoods changed. From the dead quiet of the hotel district, we entered a residential section, then made our way into the shuttered storefront quarter.

THE STAR MAN
OF KUNAYALA

Suddenly Gritzko was parking. At first it seemed that nothing was stirring, that the area was still asleep. The sun had not yet risen to erase the night. Dawn was near, I could sense the air was changing. Faintly I saw a little movement in one darkened doorway, then another. The streets seemed to be coming alive as shadowy, sunken-eyed figures in worn clothes and with tousled hair began to emerge from the darkness.

My driver, obviously at ease in this darkened netherworld, quickly set his parking brake and, without a thought, was out of the car and marching toward an empty taxi. I bolted out the door, hurrying to catch up, hoping that I would be safer with him than in the car alone. Nervously I watched the alleys and doorways for any unusual activity. Everything stayed the same.

In a flash, Gritzko was banging on the window of the cab and yelling, cursing. The scene turned surreal. Dark eyes turned on us, holding us in their ghastly grasp. Paying no attention to anything around him, Gritzko only pounded louder, totally oblivious to the terror I was in.

Then his pounding stopped. He was talking, carrying on a conversation. I thought he had gone mad and was talking to himself. I walked up for a closer look. There, sprawled out on the front seat of the small Japanese car, was a huge man. His rotund body seemed to absorb the entire area. He had been asleep. Gritzko was furious, bewildered that anyone would sleep in a car on the streets of Panama City.

Finally, the driver emerged, pulling his baggy pants high, vainly trying to get them over his impossible belly. They talked. Minutes passed. Then, flinging himself back toward the seat, he struggled to get in. His body fought back, but his weight took command. He was in, but still in a daze. He sat in a stupor, trying to orient himself.

In the meantime we had pulled up to the street corner in our car to wait for him to follow. Nothing happened. We waited. Then, the cab's lights were on and slowly the car moved in our direction. We were rolling. Gritzko was livid, more curses flew.

Hitting the main avenue, we watched our mirrors to make sure the cab was following. Within blocks we were at our destination. Quickly we unloaded our bags and placed them in the street to reload them into the cab. Turning, we saw the taxi coming, grabbed the gear, and headed further out into the street, but the taxi didn't seem to be slowing. We waved. Then yelled. Then waved frantically. It

was no use. He didn't even see us. The driver's eyes were set dead ahead. As he passed he seemed to be locked in fast forward, apparently still asleep. His taillights went on out of sight, not even braking for traffic signals.

Gritzko was uncontrollable. He raged, "Why would anyone in this frigging world want to be up at this hour and why would any frigging airline company fly at this frigging hour. The world has gone crazy."

Time was ticking away. Our departure was supposed to be only minutes away, and, I thought, here we are standing in the middle of a street with our bags in our hands.

Exchanging a few words, we decided to head on to the airport to see if the plane had been late in leaving or if there was a later flight.

Having calmed down and knowing that we had missed the flight, we drove at a more reasonable pace to the airport. When we arrived we found out that, much to my chagrin, there was a seven o'clock flight.

Gritzko was aflame. He was not amused—all that effort to get to the airport on time and there was another flight.

Immediately we raced back toward the city center to get yet another sleepy-headed and blurry-eyed cabbie. As we hurried, I thought, wait a minute. Listen to what is happening. Vickie Downey had told me for my book *Wisdom's Daughters* to be listening even without seeing with my eyes.

I spoke up, "This is not to be. There are signs here. We're not supposed to do this. We're not going to the islands. We're supposed to go someplace else. Let's cancel. Make other plans."

I relaxed. The ordeal was over. Now I could do the right thing.

Within minutes Gritzko dropped me back off at my hotel where, just a few hours ago, I had checked out. Now I was checking back in, heading back to the same room, taking my clothes off, and crawling back into the same unmade bed I had left. Barely touching the bed, I was immediately sound asleep as if nothing unusual had happened—just a bad dream about trying to get a flight to a place I was not going to in the first place.

The trip to San Blas, or Kunayala, had vaporized before my eyes. I had been hesitant to go, something just seemed to hold me back. I had thought, maybe this trip will fall through if the interpreter is late. And he was. Again the elder's words, "Words are powerful. Be careful what you ask for. Sooner or later you will get what you want. Be ready for it. It may not be what you expected."

SHADOWCATCHERS

I trembled at the thought. Yet, what I had asked for was to be able to meet with the elder I was supposed to be with. As I dragged myself out of bed, feeling worse than if I had stayed up, I prayed that I had not eliminated that chance. Now I shuddered at having to face the young Kuna men who had arranged the meeting, gone out of their way to pick up the tickets, made arrangements with radio calls to the island to secure a place for me to stay on the island.

Having put off the call until late in the afternoon, I telephoned Marcial for a meeting. After explaining what had happened, he accepted the changes without even a wave of the hand. There was no problem, he had said. "Think about going into the interior, down the Pan American Highway, into Kunayala near the Darien."

Besides, he had continued, there was an elder who was supposed to be in the city, was coming in today. Oddly enough, he was the one I was to meet with on the island. He would check on it for me. There were no guarantees, however. Everything had to be fluid, the right thing always rises.

Otencio Lopez, a young officer of the organization, met me at the door to the Kuna offices. His expression gave no hint of disgust at having gone to so much trouble for me and then having those plans fall through. He was even cheerful. I felt better. Immediately he suggested that he take me to meet his uncle, Carlos Lopez, or Inakelinya, the elder from San Ignacio. He had arrived from the island just hours earlier.

On the way, Gritzko made an illegal turn, he cursed. There was no undoing it. The police officer was ready, red lights flashing as Gritzko pulled to a stop in front of the apartment complex where Otencio's uncle waited. Before the officer was out of his car, Gritzko whispered, "You got five dollars?"

I asked, "Why? What's the five for?"

His eyes bore into me with a "You should know!" look. He said nothing, just held his palm outstretched. I dropped the five on him, and he ambled over to the patrol car and waited. After the cop finished talking to a beautiful young woman who had caught his attention and who, apparently, took priority, he descended on Gritzko. They talked, then Gritzko shook his hand. The money had been exchanged. The deal had been made and the ordeal was over.

We entered the two-story, flat-topped apartment building. A single dark-ened corridor, like a tunnel, separated the six ground-floor apartments, three on each side. A convenience-style grocery store occupied the front street-side corner. Music blared from behind one door, loud discussions came from another, an

197

THE STAR MAN
OF KUNAYALA

argument echoed through the passage fed by the acoustics of the cement-block tube from some undisclosed location.

Otencio knocked on the nondescript door at the far end of the breezeway. A barely audible "Come in," came from behind the closed door. It was the same murmured but welcoming "Come in," without anyone personally opening the door that I had heard countless times from within other Indian homes I had approached in the past.

Inside the bright, neat, knickknack-filled apartment, the venerated elder sat against a windowed wall in a straight-backed dining room chair. He was wearing what appeared to be thin, light blue shorty pajamas. Underneath the charcoal fedora perched squarely atop his head, his lack of wrinkles belied his age. The fedora was much like an ill-fitting crown, but symbolically portrayed authority and pomp. His weathered and worn leathery barefeet, however, spoke volumes of the miles he had traveled in his eighty years.

With much dignity and little overt reaction, he said, "Ask me what you want to know. I will try to answer. But don't you try to change one single word of mine. You write only what I say. Not one single word different."

At first there was confusion. Two interpreters stood between Inakelinya and me. It had to be that way. Earlier I had been told that when a wise man talked, he always had an interpreter. There were two Kuna languages, the vulgar one, or the language of everyday use, and the sacred. The elder would, in talking of spiritual matters, use the sacred, then the interpreter would translate it into the language of everyday use. Since Inakelinya was one of only three men comprising the Kuna tribunal, his secretary usually translated all of his words. Today, Otencio stood in.

Still it was perplexing. Otencio translated from Kuna into Spanish, Gritzko translated from Spanish into English. Then, the process was reversed. Although separated by language, I liked Inakelinya at once. He was tough, tough as nails, but he was kind. Above all he was gentle.

If there had been a barrier, it fell instantly, after translation, when I said, "I want to talk about God."

Inakelinya didn't hesitate. He started talking. "Before I die I must pass this knowledge on. The young people are not picking it up. Maybe by telling others, it will keep it alive. Someday those who were young will read it and search for more. So this will be good to tell.

"By telling you, others after I die will be able to hear this and that will carry it on."

With a sigh, as if something had been completed, he added, "That will free me of my obligation." Then came the bomb, along with his impish smile, the seriousness of it immediately branded into my mind: "It will be yours."

Then, Inakelinya began talking.

The History of Ibeorgun

Ibeorgun—that means golden orb—Ibeorgun was sent by God to teach men the way they have to live because in the past, brother would not recognize brother. Man did not have any regulations or any laws. So Ibeorgun was sent by God to teach men how to live.

When Ibeorgun came down there was disorder, there was chaos here. There were ten different people speaking ten different languages and they couldn't understand each other. There were fifteen different races then before Ibeorgun came down—among them my ancestors. We were being humiliated and lived in slavery by these other races.

I was fascinated, wanting the meeting to continue, but recognized that he was stopping it for now. As we shook hands, he held the grip longer than necessary, almost in an attempt to steady me. He started talking again, something else was on his mind.

"Tomorrow you're going into Kunayala?" he asked, not waiting for an answer. "You know I've got to go there tomorrow, too. We could go together. If I could go with you, it would save me a twelve-hour bus trip."

I was overjoyed. What an honor to be traveling with such a person. I gladly responded, "Yes, of course. There is plenty of room. You are welcome."

He was not finished. "I have a secretary. He must go, too."

No problem, I thought. I could get a larger vehicle.

"My secretary has a wife. I would like for her to come. Otencio should come and Enrique, from the organization."

Now I knew why he was trying to steady me. I needed the balance as I tried to figure how many people would be coming and how large a car I would need. There was his interpreter, my translator, his secretary and his wife, the organization's representative, my friend Don, and myself. I came up with eight. Eight! And I would need a four-wheel drive vehicle to handle the terrain.

Inakelinya, smiling up at me from chest level, tapped my shoulder, more a knowing pat, then added, "You give me this trip, I will give you what you want."

Now his smile was a grin. He knew he had driven a hard bargain. He and I laughed, knowing that it was no bargain at all. What he wanted to tell me would be told anyway, he had already made up his mind. I knew what he wanted to say couldn't be bargained away anyway. We understood each other. Our rapport had been established, possibly before we had ever met.

Inakelinya knew things, things that came to him from another source. He was a wise man, born with abilities, and recognized for them by his people. He was the Masar Igar, or strong leader, *masar* meaning "tree" or "strong," and *igar* "the way" or "leader."

Walking down the building's bleak hallway on my way out, I whirled. It hit me. Had I gone on to the island and not listened to the voice within, I would have been on a three-day trip, and returned with nothing. The elder there was Inakelinya. He was the one I had to see, the only one. Nothing could have been done without him, but he would have been in Panama City. Therefore, I would have completely missed him. The words of Leon Shenandoah came to me, "Only one path. Got to follow it even if you can't see it. Only path you got."

Now I fretted; getting a four-wheel drive vehicle large enough to comfortably carry eight people troubled me.

According to all the Indians I had ever known, there was an attitude common among them that there should be no worry, just peace, because there is a plan—even if you cannot see it. I was not at peace. Reality, or my perception of reality had disturbed my peace. Most four-wheel drives I had seen would seat only four or five people. I needed one large enough for eight.

The Great Spirit must have been watching. A call to the rental car agency had been positive, a four-wheel drive was available. No one discussed size. I decided to take my chance. What I ended up with would be what we would use.

Much to my surprise, without having planned it, the four-wheel drive was large, big enough to seat eight. It would work, even if three had to sit on tiny jump seats that dropped from the side and faced each other in the back of the vehicle. It would be tight, but it would work.

I had pressed that we would be leaving early, which, of course, didn't happen. Still, we were only minutes late when we arrived at the apartment where Inakelinya was staying. He was waiting, standing outside with his secretary and his secretary's wife. He was eager to get on the road.

If there had been a barrier, it fell instantly, after translation, when I said, "I want to talk about God."

Soon we were weaving through the streets of Panama City on the way to Kunayala. On the outskirts of the city, the paved road came to an abrupt end, just beyond the military checkpoint. As we bumped off the asphalt, dust began to boil, and the ruts, made from huge trucks during heavy rains, bounced us up and down, to and fro. We were entering the untamed territory of settlers, loggers, developers, exploiters. It was the last remaining gap in the overland route between Panama and Colombia that would someday connect the Americas.

It had been thirteen years since I had been in the area and traveled this section of the Pan American Highway. Then it had truly been a wilderness, the most pristine wilderness in the world. Only a few settlers had started moving in to fuel the race of exploitation.

Then the road had been just a narrow dirt strip cut out of untouched virgin forests. The mountains could hardly be seen just off the road, hidden by monstrous trees. Now the hills loomed naked, rugged, and ragged with peaks that seemed to scream from the loss of their foliage coverings. Pastures, as far as the eye could see, combed the landscape with tall grasses unknown to the area only a decade ago.

Then, thatched-roof huts were just being erected to house the settlers. Now concrete block houses replaced the huts. Entire villages had appeared. Restaurants and grocery stores had become common.

I closed my eyes and remembered. I was again traveling the muddy, deeply rutted road. It was active with trucks, colonials, and with straw-hatted workers astride horses. Smoke billowed as fires flamed from the slashing and burning. Everyone was staking a claim, hoping to make a fortune. Looking for gold. It was the frontier.

Now, heavy trucks were still rolling with wood from deeper south in the Darien, but most of the logging semis had given way to long-bedded beer trucks. Frontier compounds had been replaced with more manicured yards, even lawns in some places. Electricity ran deep into the interior.

The Kuna had been pushed off much of their land as they struggled to maintain their culture in the face of the destruction of their world.

I asked Inakelinya if we could talk. He said, "Maybe tonight."

I laughed, "What if I'm not with you tonight?"

Then he laughed, knowingly.

"I don't want whatever I'm saying for you to get twisted in any way . . ."

The Story of Oloniginya

Many times the Kuna have been named as savage Indians. We don't deny this conception.

Prior to this there were wild Indians, savages. It was a different kind of people. They were called Bugui-Bugui. These Bugui-Bugui people were also cannibals, they were feeding themselves out of the blood of their own people. These Bugui-Bugui were also our enemies. We had to fight and liberate ourselves from these people. To be able to free ourselves from these savages, Oloniginya had to really make a war against these people.

THE STAR MAN
OF KUNAYALA

Oloniginya was born in the jungle in the place where the rivers are born. His mother conceived him with a father who came from the stars. This was known because Oloniginya once said, "I am conceived by a father from the stars. My name means 'Father from the stars,' and he is going to help me fight this war."

His grandparents took his mother away to the place where the rivers are born, because they were hiding from their enemies, the Bugui people, who were killing them. There were no men, no visits, nobody.

While Oloniginya's father was working in the jungle, the girl was staying at home alone. Her father told her, "You are staying alone, because in this place there are no bad people. There are only rabbits and deer, which are good." The old man never knew that she was receiving visits from her friend from the stars.

Tradition says that when this man from the stars visited her, he gave her some seeds. He said if she buried the seeds in the proper place, then later he would give her the possibility of collecting other things. He actually visited her twice, and her father was already becoming suspicious about it. So, the man from the stars told her, "Tell your father to go to a certain spot in the river and he will be able to collect a lot of shrimps.

"When he asks you, 'How do you know?' Tell him that you dreamed this."

So the old man went to the river the next day because she told him, and he collected really a lot of shrimps. Eventually, as time went by, the old man realized that she was pregnant. He was very mad and very upset, and said, "How did it happen? With whom? Obviously you cannot just have this baby."

She answered, "Look, this baby came because you didn't take very good care of me. You used to leave me alone and for this reason this child is my own. He is going to be born. I want him."

When the baby was born, there were many manifestations from nature. The heavens thundered and the rivers flooded. So the old man said, "These manifestations may mean damnation."

He wanted to throw the baby into the river. He was about to do this when two women showed up and said, "Look at what you are doing. He is just a baby. He's just a child. If you don't want him, we will take him from you. Just leave him for a short while and then he's going to be grown up, be older and then we will take him." So he decided to keep the baby.

As time went by, the girl told her father how the baby was conceived. The father realized that it was his own mistake of leaving her alone that caused her to have the baby.

So the baby began growing up and everyone realized that he was growing faster than a normal child. That really astonished everyone.

As the child was growing up, one day he asked the grandfather, "Could it be true that there are only us four people in this world?" He was living with his grandfather, grandmother, and his mother.

He said, "It can't be. See, every time I go to the hill, I get to the top and I see on the horizon, I see many trees. So if there were only four people, there would only be four trees. There are thousands of trees, so there are more people, thousands of people. Since there are many trees, they also serve many purposes." He pointed out, "These trees are good for this, and these trees are good for these other things."

From that the people started to develop a system of medicine.

The old man realized that the child was somebody very wise. Eventually he had to confess to his grandson that there were other people down the river. He explained to him, as well, that his people were being murdered and isolated by this other race.

So, one day Oloniginya said, "There is also another tree, and this tree is good for making arrows." From then on they began to fight for the territory. Eventually the grandfather was collecting cures and medicines from the trees that the child told him about. He also started making arrows from a special tree the child had told him about.

War and Celebration

Before long they decided to return to their hometown. Oloniginya told the people to begin making ready a celebration that would be the beginning of a war.

So he ordered two things. One thing for making the war and one thing for making the celebration. They also built these fences with holes in between so they could fire their arrows through the holes in the fences. So the people started making the drinks called chicha and the people asked him, "But why are we making arrows and chicha? Why are we making all these arrows and all these drinks at the same time?"

He said, "We are going to make a big party and we invite all the enemies. We are going to ask them to bring their girls. The girls will sit with the young boys and the young boys will try to get the information out of them about how they live, where do they sleep, how do they sleep, and all the information about the way that they live."

Oloniginya instructed all his people and then he told the elders, "You will not drink. You will pretend you are drinking, but you will not drink. These other people will drink because they like it but they will need to see that you are drinking.

"In the morning when the girls ask about their parents, you will tell them that their parents went to another town to have another celebration because they will remember their people liked to drink very much."

The celebration began and the girls began telling the boys all the details on how they sleep. They said, "The men sleep during the day, and they work and hunt at night. They hide themselves by hanging from ropes in the trees, and sometimes they sleep with their face downwards."

When the Bugui people, the bad people, started to get drunk, they were all killed by the Kunas.

Ibeorgun, the One Sent by God

It is important to understand the beginning of the Kuna.

Ibeorgun, the one who was sent by God, came down to tell everyone that each person is your brother and your sister and these are the sons. The sons have to respect the older ones and, also, the older ones have to respect the younger ones.

In those days there was chaos, there was no order, so Ibeorgun had to create order.

The Creation of the Congress House

After the war was ended, they had to create the society, the Kuna society. That's why Ibeorgun was important. He was the First Being to teach us how to build our social structure. Also, because the people lived in

"Oloniginya was born in the jungle in the place where the rivers are born. His mother conceived him with a father who came from the stars."

the outdoors, he taught the people how to build the first house. Then, he told them to build a bigger house and call it the House of the Congress.

He instructed the people to get together, reunite, and choose some-body to lead them and maintain order in the community. So they orga-nized all the social administration of the community: the chief, the speakers, the local politics, everybody.

From this they derived three authorities: the sahila—the chief; the speaker—who is the one who translates what the chief has to say to the people; and the third one, whose name means "stick"—who is in charge of organizing and maintaining order.

There are two languages. One is the sacred language and the other one we call the vulgar one, which is used in everyday talk.

Ibeorgun explained to them that in the big house, the Congress House, they have to have two hammocks. These two hammocks repre-sent the material world and the spiritual world.

First the sahila, the chief, will sing and pray from the spiritual ham-mock. The message from the spiritual world to the material world is given first through the sahila and then to the people. The hammock has to be in the center of the building, because this represents the heart of man, which is in the middle of his body. In the same way, the heart of spirituality is, also, in the center of this building.

So the people elected the different chiefs and the different people who were in charge of something. There was a person who was in charge of making chicha, the drink. There was the person who was in charge of cleaning the roads, the highways.

Ibeorgun told each that "This will be your task. This will be your equipment, and these are the people who will work with you. You have to have them close by all the time."

Ibeorgun taught each how to maintain this team of people, because, he said, "You cannot take the ship of the state, the ship of the community, by yourself. You need this group of people working with you."

So he instructed that the Congress House must be built by everyone. He taught, "One day you will work in this house. The next day there will be other people working. There will be parties in this house when there is something to celebrate, and there will be sorrow when there is something to be sorry about.

"I didn't come here to stay, I have to go back," Ibeorgun said. "I only came here to give you some directives on how to do things."

Time Before Columbus

In our history the amount of people that existed at this time was so huge that we counted them as rivers of people. Every river was inhabited and had its own civilization.

Our world was not exactly like an empire, but it behaved as if it was. It had a main city or a capital called Paya. It is still there and it is a small Kuna town. None of its past glory exists, except the people there still use the old Kuna language.

The Kuna were not the only ones in this world. There were people of different colors. There were very light people like the color of balsa and people with darker skins. Other people were like the color of the soil. We were warned about these by Ibeorgun. He said these people would visit us one day. Ibeorgun said these people had a different sea from us. Their wind was cooler than ours and their sea was braver. It was not as peaceful as ours.

Although we didn't have any maps, we knew our land configuration in the area and that we were inside of a big bay. That is why we are living in a very privileged place. When all the hurricanes and bad weather comes, we are protected even by other bad weather conditions. That makes ours a very privileged place.

We knew all the places by the right name. All the hydrography, all the information about the river was known to us in those days. And the geography of Panama in those days was the geography of our rivers because the rivers were very much tied into our history. That is the pride of the Kuna history that we maintained.

The only weapons that existed for us were arrows, lances, stones of different shapes with sharp points on sticks. That was all that we had. And we used them mostly for hunting.

The Neles

Christopher Columbus claimed that he discovered us. We existed so many years before him that there is no explanation for that. The arrival of

Christopher Columbus was very, very many years after Ibeorgun came. After Ibeorgun we have had nine Neles, nine wise men who were in between. That would put the first Nele here about two thousand years ago. When Columbus arrived, the ninth Nele, or wise man, was ruling. The name of that wise man was Igua Salibler. There have only been ten Neles in the history of the Kuna.

We may be talking about the period of nine hundred to a thousand years, because if there are ten Neles and each of them lived for about one hundred years, ten Neles at a hundred years would be about nine hundred to one thousand years.

Iberogun warned us that these white people, Christopher Columbus, would arrive. And these ten Neles would come to assist Iberogun to complete the work he started and taught us. So we knew that they were coming and these people would aid Iberogun. My ancestors were expecting them. The Neles were being expected also.

The Neles' Powers

Neles are ordinary human beings born on this earth. The father of the first Nele came from the stars, but he was born on this earth, here. Each of the ten Neles was actually the son of a person from the stars and a human being from this earth.

There are some Neles still alive, but they are different. They don't have all the powers that prior Neles had. Those people had very special powers.

The Neles today, the ones that are alive now, they have certain powers. They can cure certain diseases and things, but the other Neles, those ten people, they had special powers. They might just be sitting there and they might kill you or they might make the thunder come down. They had really powerful magical powers.

To begin with, Neles were not just men. They were also females. Actually there were twelve in all, but three of them died. One of them was dead before he was born but only nine of them reigned.

The Neles' Knowledge

Each of these Neles had their own knowledge that developed through investigation, a sense of finding out things. For instance, one of them delegated his life to understanding nature, the trees, how they breed, how they live. Another Nele delegated himself to understand how the world was created, how the people were created. Each specialized in something.

One of these Neles had investigated the sea. Pai Liver studied the anatomy of the human body and medicine, but mostly the human anatomy. Another Nele started the study of the sun and the stars. His name was Ologana Kunkilele. Uagibler was another Nele who specialized in the world of the birds. He said birds had similar organization as we have. They have their own boss, their own sahila, and they have their own house, the main house in which they live.

The Nele is born with wisdom. The Nele is a genius because he is very young when he starts talking about things that the others don't understand. At about ten years old he starts talking about philosophy and things that no one has taught to him and yet, still he knows. Everybody notices that he is a Nele. He's a wise person.

There's only one or two at a time. It takes quite a long time between one Nele and the next one to be born. Neles are a very rare occurrence and only once every donkey's year do you have one of these Neles.

Inakelinya stopped abruptly, leaving only the silence. No one said anything. I just waited, not knowing if there would be more. Still he said nothing. He was deep in thought. I considered breaking the pause, but I held back.

I looked out at the scenery, thinking that something would come to mind to jump start the conversation. My mind was blank. Then, Inakelinya warned: "Don't think too much. Don't use your brain so much because I don't want to tell you everything. I can't tell you everything."

I had been admonished. He had touched my weak point. It was true that my mind was at work, even when I was quiet. I took his scolding to heart, realizing he was probably, at that very moment, hearing my thoughts. I let him decide if he wanted to say more. It wasn't long before he was ready again. There was so much more I needed to hear, craved to understand, I breathed a sigh of relief when he began again.

Baths with Plants

Since I was born, I have had many baths immersed in special medicine, good medicine. I'll use an analogy. When you are born and you are so shortsighted, you have to go to a doctor and get your glasses. Well, in a Nele's world, in a symbolic way, to have your glasses really means to have a bath with magic plants so you can open your eye, so your eyesight becomes even better and sharper. You have many baths in the medicine to continue to sharpen your eyesight. I have had many baths, immersed in good medicine many times.

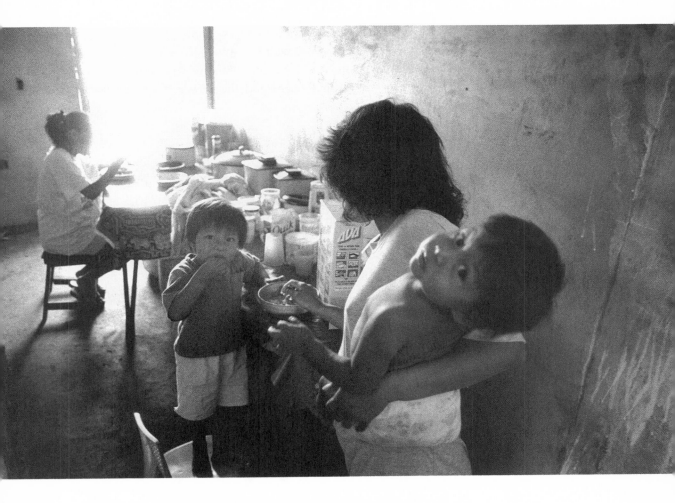

"Ibeorgun, the one who was sent by God, came down to tell everyone that each person is your brother and your sister and these are the sons."

In the baths with the plants, there is contact with more than just the wisdom of the plants, there is contact with the spirits. They don't touch you, but they talk to you. You can hear them talking to you. When you get one of these baths your mind opens and the power of the plants comes through you.

The Nuchu

The Nele talks to his Nuchu. The Nuchu is like a dummy made out of the skin of the tree. So the Nele has this image made out of bark and through this Nuchu he communicates with the spirit.

The Nele doesn't cure anybody. The man who cures the people is the medicine man, but the Nele tells the medicine man what to do to cure the person. He uses the Nuchu to make a diagnosis. The Nele keeps an eye on the ill person, and he can tell the medicine man if he is doing the right thing or if he will have to change the treatment. He tells how well or how bad the treatment is working.

The Nele speaks to the spirit and the healer looks at the symptoms. The Nele does it through the spiritual world, while the medicine man does it through the material world.

A Nele is a person who knows when there's going to be an eclipse of the moon or the sun. He also knows when there's going to be an earthquake or any other kind of natural disaster. Now we have a calendar that can tell us about eclipses, but previously it was the Nele who knew about these things.

Ibeorgun warned that when people start losing their respect for human life, when people stop caring for their brother, for their neighbor, when people have lost all these values, there will be a great change. Those changes are done through disasters. When a disaster happens, civilizations fall and the whole cycle starts all over again.

At the beginning of that cycle, you can just tell by looking at it that something is going to happen because you can see it. It's not hard to tell that something is coming. When the sea comes and invades, like a tidal wave, it will start in certain areas first but eventually it will effect the big civilizations. Some have already experienced these tidal waves in the late 1800s. I have talked to them.

In the last century there were tidal waves in Kunayala, San Blas. Several islands disappeared. It was just a runner of what is to come. An elder told me to stop this from happening by continuing to say thanks to God, every time. He warned if man forgets about God and the world, the earth will forget about the man. If man will keep saying to God, "Hey, thank you," for all that he is receiving, this will not have to happen.

We are already living in those times in which man is forgetting everything. He just doesn't care. It's a very materialistic world.

We always insist to our people to always go to the Congress House to give thanks to God to maintain the contact with God. That's why we keep saying this.

Good and Evil Spirits

Sometimes there are spirits, similar to angels, called Baliwitur, and these are spirits that come down and talk to Indians, but you don't see them. You just listen to them.

There are, also, evil spirits who try to stop you from communicating with God. There are people who are influenced by these spirits. They steal and do bad things. There are young people, those who take drugs or participate in that kind of activities. They are people who are influenced by evil spirits. Among us, it is becoming very bad because it's spoiling people's heads, really screwing them up.

The evil spirits are taking over the world. You can tell that everyday. There are more and more people involved in these activities. We do the best we can to help other people. But people who take drugs have to have money, and to have money, they are willing to do almost anything. So money is also a materialistic way of making people go their own way. We are doing the best we can, but that doesn't seem to be enough.

God created and left us only the good, but the evil one also exists and he has his own kingdom. Although God won the fight against the evil, the forces of evil still exist and haven't been completely defeated. Evil has exactly the same powers as God. Evil and good exists and they both have exactly the same powers. God won over evil in the battle, but he didn't destroy evil completely. It is very similar to the Christian tradition that

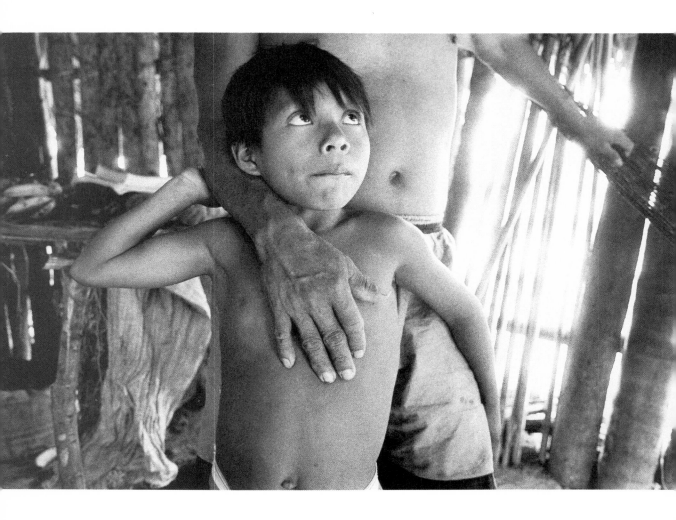

the devil is working and it is also in our tradition that the devil takes the image of the snake.

Again similar is the belief that the devil was somebody that was working with God and eventually he wanted to have more powers than God and that's why he was expelled.

Ibeorgun is the son of God. In a way Ibeorgun is like Christ, but Ibeorgun came from the stars and Christians say that Christ came from heaven. When we say the stars, we also mean that place, a different world, that exists in the sky. That's why we say from the stars. The word heaven is more modern.

There is only one spirit, every person has a spirit. In dreams you can make your spirit to travel and communicate with other spirits. I have traveled to the United States, I have been there before, but I haven't made a visit there. I dreamed this. The wise men told me to dream of traveling to a different world means that you are going to have a very long life.

The Battle Between the Neles

There is no more magic in the Kunas' world. No more. That is because the Neles abused the power they had. For instance, they have three, four, five, even six wives. They were confronting each other to see who had more power. I will tell you how they were punished for this.

The Nele Deigun was a very powerful man. He was also very strong. He got a lot of magic and he had a lot of women. He started to take revenge against people who didn't like him. So other Neles decided they had to get rid of him, but they couldn't because he knew everything everyone was thinking.

He killed the parents of a girl, because if he wanted a girl for marriage and the parents refused to give her to him, he just killed them. He could talk to nonmaterial things like a chair, table, something that wasn't alive. If you said anything wrong about him, you would die instantly because he would know and seek revenge.

Another Nele wanted to get rid of this guy, so he went to the woods and started collecting medicine. He could talk to the trees and the trees told him, "Hey, you can't get rid of him like this. This is not the way. You have to get all the clever people, all the Neles, and they have to go to the river where the water flows fast and talk about this and make your plans. If you talk, the wind will take your words and he will hear, but the river will be like a lion and wash them out—the roar of the rapids covers the words."

Deigun never found out what they talked about at this meeting at the river. What they did was plan to have a party, a big chicha, and they began making all the preparations for this party.

While this party was taking place, all the Neles, the good and the bad Neles, participated. Why? Because if they did not participate Deigun would suspect. So they participated in this and when Deigun arrived with his eight wives, the good Neles and the warriors were watching him.

There was this special road used only by the Neles. As they were leaving, the good Neles began killing all the bad Neles, but when they tried to force the string in the arch, the bowstring snapped off. The only exception was for Ibeler, he got the magic so the string in his arch didn't rip. So he got to fire. But he didn't kill Deigun. There were four trained warriors who did the killing.

Deigun was drunk. So when he started walking on this road, he was next to his wives. He had four on one side and four on the other side. Although he was drunk the strings in the arch of the other Neles were ripping because he was that powerful, except for Ibeler's arch.

When they killed him, Deigun said, "Oh, you were ahead of me because I was going to do the same to you."

That's what Deigun said.

They had to cut him in eight pieces and bury him in eight different places because he was so powerful. If they had left him in one piece, he would come back to life again.

In the burial they had to use a lot of hot spices to cover all his parts, then bury him. Only then could they make sure he wouldn't get together again.

When they cut him into pieces, he was still alive. He was still complaining and screaming and crying, because he was still alive.

He was one of the most powerful Neles that has ever existed. He was such a powerful man and had so much magic, but he abused so much of it that he had to be destroyed by the magic of the other guys.

After they killed Deigun they made another party, another chicha; chicha is a drink. Those that survived killing Deigun, they came back.

When all these Neles came to this party, the warriors made them sit all in one row. They came with their lances and placed them on the floor with strength. They told them, "We killed Deigun because he was evil. If you behave like that, if you use your power in the wrong way, we'll do the same thing to you."

The moral is never get eight wives.

Finally after forging streams, dodging deep ruts, and being shaken to the bone, we arrived at the Kuna village of Ibedi, a community of about one thousand people, on the banks of the Mandungandi River—translated "river with lots of plantains and bananas."

Immediately Inakelinya was greeted by the village chief, Jose Oller, and taken to the Congress House as a diplomatic courtesy. Inside, benches lined the walls, hammocks of differing sizes hung in the center. Inakelinya took a seat, the seat of honor, in the center.

Within minutes an older woman entered with a bowl filled with a black liquid. Inakelinya drank first, then his secretary, and next it was offered to all the others gathering to meet with him.

Otencio, knowing that it was time to leave Inakelinya to his duties, asked if I would like to join him for a tour of the village. I accepted.

Walking down the path between the huts, I was arrested by an unusual odor, a foreign aroma. My nostrils flared in rebellion. The scent floated on the ever so light breeze stirring the stifling heat and seemed to be coming from everywhere at once.

Passing an open door, a Kuna excitedly rushed out.

"Come in," he demanded, taking my arm and pulling me in. I couldn't resist. What seemed to be just another house turned out to be a great hall. A group of men huddled to one side. Behind them huge earthenware jars, almost the size of vats, lined the wall. Some of the jars seemed ancient, large cracks creasing their robust curves and making them useless. At the far end of the line newer ones commanded more attention from the revelers. One after another was taking a gourdlike cup, dipping it deep, and returning to join the others—all the while sipping the powerful liquid.

Across the room, row upon row of hammocks filled fully half of the dingy meeting house. All hung empty—all except one. Its occupant was out cold, totally oblivious to his surroundings.

At the far end, a woman, the wife of one of the men cavorting near the vat, bent over red hot coals circled by river stones, cooking. A monkey on a rope screamed in anguish at her whenever anyone approached, violating its territory.

By the time I realized I was in the village chicha hall, a group of men had surrounded me with a worn wooden bowl filled with the aromatic chicha.

"Drink," I was invited, as a group of men broke out into song, chants in the Kuna sacred language.

"Drink, have some, try it," the bowl nearly up to my lips. The men pressed closer, eagerly awaiting my decision.

I knew I really had little choice. There were too many of them, all of their faces crushing in tighter and tighter, intent on seeing my reaction. I hesitated, they coaxed. We were eye to eye. Their breath flooded me with an intoxicating wind.

I relented and drank. They laughed. My lips flared, my throat became a torch, and my stomach burned. I staggered, my body on fire. Again they laughed

SHADOWCATCHERS

My lips flared, my throat became
a torch, and my stomach burned.
I staggered, my body on fire.

and continued laughing all the way back to their wooden perches, quickly falling into a chorus of song. I had been initiated.

The flames lingered and my lips continued to burn long into the night.

Later, nearing the chicha house, voices again rose in unison above the thatched houses and drifted along the footpaths. With the day lowering into dusk, they grew more intense and, with each verse, louder. This time my passing went unnoticed.

I had been taken into one of the thatched-roof, earth-floor homes. It took some time for my eyes to adjust to the dim light, having come in from the bright, tropical sun. Slowly the one-room structure, serving as living room, bedroom, kitchen, and all-purpose family gathering area, became brighter. In the middle, nestled against the single, hand-hewn supporting beam, a box of wooden figurines caught my attention. Leaning against each other, stacked tightly together, the images looked out into the room from every direction. I was intrigued, so I moved closer for a better look.

227

THE STAR MAN
OF KUNAYALA

"They don't like to be disturbed," I was told. "They're touchy that way. They sleep until they are needed. Some emergency. When help is needed."

I squatted next to them. I started to ask if I could photograph them, stopped and thought about it, and then, hesitantly, I asked.

"It's okay, but you'd better not. They don't like to be messed with. You can if you want to, but something will happen to your camera, to your film."

"With the Nuchus we have a ceremony. We have a smoke. We smoke a pipe. The ceremony is done to find out what is going on in the atmosphere, what's going on.

"Last week we did this ceremony to find out what was going on, because there were so many people ill for different reasons. There was disease everywhere. So we did this smoke session."

I photographed anyway and thought nothing more about it.

Weeks later, after returning to the United States, I arranged to process my film. Jokingly I told a friend, as we developed the rolls together, about the warning I had been given. We found it mildly humorous.

When the film was finished, I looked over the rolls hanging in the drying cabinet. Something had gone wrong. Almost every roll was affected. There were tiny spots scattered over every strip. None of the spots ruined the rolls completely, none of the important images, but, nevertheless, they were there reminding me of powers I had been told about but took lightly, apparently too lightly. Mohawk medicine woman Cecilia Mitchell had said, "Just because you can't see something doesn't mean it doesn't exist."

When we left the village for the trip back to Panama City, Inakelinya stayed to tend to his official business. In our parting conversation, Otencio stated, "My uncle told you more, in a little time, than I have ever heard him tell outsiders. More than he has told me. He must feel that now is really the time to put it out.

"I am both jealous and surprised. That's joke and truth. I am jealous is a joke. I am surprised is the truth."

Earlier in the day, I had asked Inakelinya if he was a Nele. He had answered in a vague way. Now I asked Otencio if his uncle was a Nele. All he would say was, "He's a very great man. You must know," and nothing more.

Later, while driving back toward Panama City, I thought about Inakelinya's words as we left him behind in Ibedi.

"I am telling you only true things," he had said. "Perhaps others will hide these things from you because Indian people are jealous about this information. Mostly they don't like giving these things away to white people, but what can I do? I'm giving you in my very best faith all this information so you let people know, because I know eventually people will know.

"In all this region I am recognized by all the people as the one with the highest knowledge about these things. That is why I can give you this information, and I do so willingly. I have reasons.

"If I could only think that all this information is going to be transmitted after I am dead, I will be very grateful because in that way I won't feel all this responsibility to make sure it continues to live on. If you repeat what I have told you, you will be doing part of my work. I have to give it away so others will someday hear it.

"I am very glad you came, because this seems to be a happy reunion. I am also sad because we probably won't see each other any more. So, I am hoping that part of this wisdom also serves you in some way."

BOOK 3

THE JOURNEY CONTINUES

18

VISITED BY ANGELS

We left on the night of the full moon. All that lay before us was the ghostly glow of the mountains and a black ribbon of a road. It was nearing midnight, and the now almost deserted, foggy Carolina highway snaked out of sight into the inky, gently rolling hills of an ebony abyss. In a race against time, my son, a doctor friend, and I took to the Blue Ridge backroads to link up with Interstate 40, cross the Great Smokies and head due west across the continent. Bound for the Mexican Pacific, we had three to four days of near round-the-clock driving to get to the coast for our appointed rendezvous with Leandis, when he would introduce us to his mentor.

Months earlier the aging Leandis had said, "I want you to come with me. I will take you to my teacher."

When I last saw him, I had gone as far as I could go both psychologically and spiritually. So I had returned home and followed his instructions to take a long, hard look at myself. On parting, he said we would meet again, reaching across the gulf of despair I had created for myself to lead me to a deeper understanding of spiritual realities, maybe even sanity. My shadows, those illusive demons of past experiences, had risen back up with my remembering them. They plagued me to the extent that I was becoming paralyzed again. I realized that I had become so blinded that I could not see that what the elders had told me was meant to help me, even if the ancient knowledge was coming from their culture. All I was hearing, over and over, were stories and more stories.

When I had asked Leandis about all the stories Indians tell, he said, "Some of my people get upset that I would tell you our stories. They say I'm giving something away. I laugh at them. I tell them that to the non-Indian our stories are just stories, they will never understand them, anyway. They're just stories. But to us the secret formulas of medicine are hidden in some. In others, the meaning of life is in them. Important lessons in all of them—story lessons—so you won't have to learn from experiences.

"Hear the story, change your life. Or, go out and have your experiences. Harder lessons that way.

"So, I say to everybody, 'They're just stories,' and I laugh. 'They're just stories. Don't mean nothing.'"

As much as I had heard the many stories, I had missed the teachings, too, because three questions, the same ones that hammered away at my mind during the darkness of my nightmarish depression, again arose and constantly occupied my thinking. Off and on, especially during bouts of despair, they would appear: "Who am I? Where did I come from? What am I doing here?" I felt I was going to die if I didn't get some answers.

Yet, while sliding into that encompassing twilight, with shades of depression pumping my fears to frightful heights, there was something calling me. On leaving Don Dahler in Costa Rica, I told him that there was something I had to do. My thoughts, then, were that I had to cross my own country to find something, anything, to ground me. One thing I knew, I had to find myself. I would have argued with Leandis if he had said he knew that was what I needed. But when he suggested the very same thing as a trip to his teacher, I was more than ready to accept the idea.

Back in Mexico, sitting in the shade of a blossoming tree, out of the glare of the noonday sun, he had gently injected into our casual conversation, "You may travel all over the world and obtain a knowledge of spiritual matters, but you can only find your own spirituality in your own land. That's where your world started, and that's where your roots are. Even medicine people can only help where their people are, where they come from. They have a connection there. That's the way it is. Always has been."

Then, he sent me a note that he had to go to Baja, and that he would actually travel to Charlotte. We would make the trip together. There, he had said, he would introduce me to his elder. My heart pounded, skipping beats at the prospects. Seemingly he knew more about me than I did. He knew what I needed most, or at least I wanted to think that he did. Immediately I offered to cover his expenses. Through a series of long-distance telephone conversations, the date for the trip was set.

In mounting anticipation, my overriding concern was whether I would try to get my eleven-year-old Oldsmobile in good enough condition to make the journey—its value was in its size and comfort, and that it was paid for—or rent a car. Renting a car lost out and repairing the old Olds won.

A week before the scheduled departure I took the car to Toccoa, Georgia, where my good friend Dr. James Chastain lived and practiced medicine. Since I had asked him along on the trip, he suggested I bring the car there and he would take it to his mechanic. He had indicated the rates for fixing any problems would be more reasonable. "They'll do us a good job," he said. "They have to, they're patients of mine."

I was skeptical that anything could be done to make the old car road-ready. It had been sitting idle for four or five months due to my having been told by an authorized dealership that it had a burned valve. That being the case, I knew only a valve and ring job would give me enough confidence in it to drive anywhere, much less to the opposite side of the country. It was a junker, I had thought. So I parked it in hopes that I would be able to sell it. It didn't sell. No one else wanted the clonker either.

Still, I liked the old bomb. I dreamed that one day I would again float along in it, in style, over the roughest of terrain. James, or rather his mechanics, had revived my fantasy. There was no valve problem. The car, I was told, needed a new ignition module, several sensors, the carburetor cleaned, and the carbon buildup blown out. The engine, it seemed, was in good condition—good condition for the aging icon of another era that it was.

That was all I needed to hear. "Fix the thing," I had told James, "and let's take it. Besides," I had gone on, "I'll save the rental fees. I'll save money!"

"Come get it and drive it first," he hedged on every one of many phone conversations we had concerning the repairs. "See what you think. You will have to make the decision."

A few days before departure, I went after the "Regency," as I again referred to it, and brought it back to North Carolina. "The boat floated back," I called and told him. "It's settled. Let's take it."

My peace of mind cracked. I paced and inside I raged.

But taking the trip with Leandis was not to be.

On the day before he was to arrive and we were to leave together, while I was in the hospital emergency room hooked up to IVs and a catheter from an attack of kidney stones, he called. He left a message on my answering machine that he would meet me in Mexico. That was it, nothing about where or when.

After wrestling with the worst pain I had ever experienced in my life and trying to overcome the exhaustion of the ordeal I had been through in the hospital, I panicked. What was I going to do? There was no way I could contact him to change plans or to even let him know of the condition I was in.

I had no choice. I would leave anyway. I would just follow my internal compass, because I was ready for the trip anyway. Sometime during the trip, I figured, he would try to get back in touch, and the information I needed would be relayed to me.

Warned by my doctor that I might not have passed the stone or stones and that the risks for a reoccurrence were just too high to undertake such a grueling journey, I remained unfazed. With my pain gone, I felt as good as before the attack. Besides, my son, Chris, would be going with me for support, and I would have a doctor, James, in case there were any complications.

So, my only consideration was that I had to get to Baja. It was set up and I would meet Leandis at whatever costs. Being with him, again, and sitting with his teacher was just too great an opportunity to miss.

Tingling with a sense of adventure and mystified as to actually where and how I was to meet up with Leandis, I helped Chris load the car. Believing that everything would somehow work out, one way or the other, we headed for Toccoa to pick up James. But, before we crossed the Charlotte city limits, the red light on the temperature gauge lit up.

The thermostat had seized, causing the car to overheat. There was nothing to do but seek out a mechanic to have it repaired. It was Friday afternoon in the city. Finding anyone who had the time to help was impossible. Rushing from one dealership to another, this garage to that one, I finally decided to buy the part, purchase a ratchet set, and fix it myself. In the heat of the blistering June sun, in a department store parking lot, I did just that.

Soaked to the skin with perspiration, grease up to my armpits, and after having waited for Chris to walk a mile to a parts store to get a correct gasket to replace a clerk's mistake, we took to the road—hours off schedule. Fortunately, a friend saw our distress and offered whatever help he could. His cellular phone allowed me to call my wife to inform her of our delay. She was able to contact James and relay word that we would be late.

When we arrived, he was napping in his office but ready nevertheless. Now, nothing stood in our way; the open road lay ahead.

Only an hour or so into the trip, while absently taking in the sweet fragrances of the highlands and occasionally catching glimpses of the glimmering stars through patches in the whiteouts of the valley fogs, the inside of the car suddenly flared red. It took me a minute to get my senses. Chris jerked alert, pulling up hard on the back seat. Alarmed, I squinted and turned quickly to James, on the passenger side, only to be taken by the glow of the reflection flooding his face. His expression said it all, "We've got a problem." It was then that I realized what was wrong. The car had overheated, again. The temperature gauge radiated in warning.

Immediately, the thought went through my mind, "We'll be stranded," knowing that miles lay between us and the Interstate, the only highway where there could possibly be any services available at such an hour. We slowed, continuing our climb to the crest of the hill, and as fate would have it—a miracle to us—we topped the pinnacle and found directional markers guiding us into a rest area. We all breathed a sigh of relief—at least we would not be broken down on the side of the road.

We raised the hood to find the hose connecting the radiator to the engine ballooned to a disproportionate size. A ranger pulled up alongside, cut his engine, hoisted himself from the cab of his truck and ambled over. "Got a problem?" he laughed, knowing full well the potential of the situation.

He glanced first at the hose then up at me, wide-eyed. He said nothing, then his gaze fell back to the hose, lazing there for minutes, and back up at James. Pushing his baseball cap up off his forehead, he frowned, taking a step or two backward, "I'm no mechanic! But, you can't go far like that. You still got some miles to go up to the Interstate then an exit or two to the nearest truck stop. That's the closest place open this time of night."

Chris, James, the ranger, and I huddled over the car, each on one foot with the other braced up on the front bumper of the old Olds, our heads bowed

under the hood. All four of us stared silently at the swollen rubber tube. That's when Chris started, "Should've rented a car. Told you that in Charlotte. We've already had this problem before. Now again!"

"Minor problem," James drawled, saving me for the time being, "even new ones go out. Replace it and go on. Takes a little patience, that's all. We'll make it."

The ranger piped in, "I'm no mechanic, but maybe if you let it cool and loosen the radiator cap, you can get to a station. I've done that before. Maybe it's just the thermostat, nothing more, but I'm no mechanic. Don't just take my word for it."

Time and again, one and then the other of us would take an old shirt, wrap it around our hand, and, with eyes closed tight, try to turn the cap. Water and steam would spew each time there was a hint of pressure being lessened on the overtaxed system. Frantically, with a grimace, the cap would be resealed, signaling yet another long wait.

Under his breath, but purposefully loud enough to be heard, Chris repeated, "I just knew it. We should've rented a car. Should've rented a car."

My peace of mind cracked. I paced and inside I raged. I wanted to push the car off a cliff. Right then. The nearest one. Still, I knew there was something right about making the trip in the old junker.

As I seethed, caught up in my own little war within, James squeezed the cap and turned it. It was off, the pressure had been released without too much loss of coolant. Triumphantly, he proclaimed, "Let's get going. Let's find that truck stop, find another cap, the right one, and get a damn cup of coffee."

Up on the Interstate, we found the truck stops, both of them at the same exit. Neither one had the radiator caps with the right configuration for the amount of pressure the manual called for. But we did get the coffee, coffee at each stop, and hit the road with the old cap riding loose and several containers of coolant in case of an overflow from overheating.

All night and into the next day, we stopped at rest areas and truck stops, one after the other. First it was to look for radiator caps, then for coolant. Nevertheless, we seemed to be making good time. By the time we reached Memphis, Chris was telling us of his plans to write a book about rest areas. We laughed hard, then the car died on the six-lane Interstate bypassing the city. Our laughing came to a quick halt. Three hours by the side of the road with no one stopping to help, not even the occasional police cruisers, almost dried our humor up completely. Little did we know that our troubles had barely begun.

"Take your time. There's no hurry. Go too fast, and you'll have to be slowed down. Pay attention to everything all along the way. I'll see you in Mexico."

We had little choice but to fix each problem as it arose. What was supposed to be a three- or, at the most, four-day trip across the United States turned out to take seven. After spending three days in Arkansas alone, we thought that we would never get out of the state. In all, we replaced four thermostats, two ignition modules, two coils, a distributor, three radiator caps, a radiator, a hose, and a set of plugs. The oil was changed twice, and we went through four gallons of coolant, with three more in the trunk as backups. Finally, the compressor on the air conditioner blew apart. When Chris wasn't audibly saying, "Should've rented a car," and he was repeating it over and over, a little voice in my head was.

One night in Russellville, Arkansas, after having been delivered to the nearest motel in a tow truck and having the car taken on to a garage, I called home to report in. I was told Leandis had called. My wife passed on his message, "Take your time. There's no hurry. Go too fast, and you'll have to be slowed down. Pay attention to everything all along the way. I'll see you in Mexico."

Then, after he had found out my son was along, he wanted him to know, "The trip is important for him, too. He's going to come into contact with a very strong feminine energy. It will reshape his thinking and affect his life."

There had been no indication as to where or when we would meet, nor had there been any information as to how I could contact him or he me. He was doing a good job of staying just out of reach. Yet he knew he could get me through my wife. Doubts about everything began to plague me. Everything! The entire trip began to seem crazy.

After discussing our situation and the information forwarded to us, none of us could make any sense out of any of it. We were totally in the dark and even began considering the possibility of turning back. I voiced concern. I was worn out and spoke up, "My time of working with Indians must be over. Just look how this trip is turning out. Nothing is right. Maybe we should turn back. The old man has thrown me a real curve this time." Still, I had to go on. It wasn't even a matter of choice.

By the next morning, we were ready to push on. Occasionally one of us would even crack a joke. The rest of us would chuckle, however faintly.

With the repairs completed in Russellville, and more repairs an hour or so later in Clarksville, we again ran into trouble just west of Ozark. James had been teasing Chris by asking him if he had three wishes what would they be.

Chris was prepared, his wit, as always, ever-ready, "I would want to be successful at whatever I tried to do, to have enough money to be free to do whatever I wanted, and to be able to have any woman I wanted."

Then, James said, "If you could have only two wishes, what would they be?"

Chris thought about it for just a moment, then quickly said, "I would want to have enough money to be free, and have any woman I wanted."

We all laughed and James injected the obvious question, "What if only one wish?"

Chris didn't hesitate, the comeback on the tip of his tongue, "The woman!"

As we roared, the temperature light came on. Fortunately for us, a rest area was in sight, and we rolled into a space in the parking lot next to a yellow 1973 Mustang, paint peeling and rusting. The hood on the battered Ford was raised, and, inside, the backseat was packed nearly to the roof with clothes. A pool of greenish liquid flooded the asphalt in front of the car. We felt the pain of our own troubles as we imagined the emotional upheaval the travelers of the vacant car must have been experiencing.

By the time I could pull the release lever, get out of the car, and raise the hood, water was already backing up into the overflow reservoir. Disgusted, I sat down on the curb to wait for the engine to cool. Chris and James stayed in the car for a while sipping soft drinks we had picked up at a fast-food joint after repairs a few miles back down the road. Then they wandered aimlessly around the car, nervously passing jokes back and forth.

In time, the vacuum of the motor's cooling system began sucking the fluid back into the radiator. Testing the temperature, I started the car. The red warning light was out, leading me to believe I could make it to the next service station down the Interstate.

Backing out, after having scrambled back into the old tank, James said, "Wonder what about these people?" his long finger slowly drifting in an aim toward the ailing used-up Mustang.

I looked over at the car beside me, then down at a picnic shelter where a weary young woman and a little girl played, the obvious occupants since no other cars were in the area. "Can I possibly be ready for this?" I said to myself.

Turning first to James, then to Chris, I searched for any hint of direction. James was silent, but Chris seemed eager. He had already taken notice of the older of the two. Reluctantly, I yielded, "We can't leave without at least asking if they need help, now can we?"

Putting the car in park, I opened the door, stood halfway outside on one leg, and yelled out over the din of passing eighteen-wheelers, "You need any help?"

Nodding a quick, "Yes," the young woman grabbed the hand of the child and took out across the field toward the restrooms. After a few leaps, she shouted back gleefully in youthful ecstasy, "Wait! I'll get my mother and sister. Wait!"

Within minutes Toni, a Mexican-American–Cherokee, and her three daughters came running at breakneck speed down the hill. She was chattering long before she ever arrived, "I had just gone to try to talk a trucker into helping us. I didn't know what I was going to do. Been in Arkansas almost three days. Now we're stranded. We just had repairs made. Cost a fortune. Took all the money I had to get to my parents in California. Just left my husband in North Carolina who was doing things he shouldn't have been doing. I had to get away, planned this trip for a long time. He doesn't know where we are. That's just as well. I don't want him to know. Thinks we're probably with friends 'cause he knew this old car wouldn't make it anywhere.

"When Michelle told me you were here offering help, I had just prayed to God, 'You got us here. You can't leave us alone. You got to help us. It's in your hands. What are you going to do about it!' And here you are."

On and on she talked. Finally, we had to calm her to get to the bottom of her trouble and decide what could be done to help solve the problem.

Traveling into Ozark and returning with Lucky, a local mechanic, we offered what snacks we had while Toni's vehicle was being worked on. Acknowledging that they had not eaten all day, the bewildered family readily accepted our invitation and eagerly dug into the junk food as if it were a gourmet dinner.

Hours passed. At long last, after working as fast as he could, Lucky tightened the remaining loose bolts. His work was finished. With the sun riding the highway just above the western horizon, we began to say our good-byes and pile into our own cars. Bending around the left front fender, Toni stopped, whirling

"To my way of thinking, my parents, my momma always used to say, 'Put it in God's hands. When you get real tired of it, put it in God's hands. There has to be a reason for it.'"

back around as Michelle and Tanya struggled to crawl into the little Ford's back seat. Not knowing how best to say it, she blurted out, "We could follow each other toward California. That way we could help each other if something else happens. You've had trouble, too. We could help each other," and she giggled uneasily, afraid she would be turned down.

For two days we traveled together before parting outside of Amarillo. Chris was in heaven. His complaining had ceased, his wish had come true. Michelle and her younger sister, spared the body-twisting confines of the Mustang's cramped quarters, had joined him in the back seat of the Oldsmobile.

At each stop, as she felt freer, Toni shared more and more of her and her family's life story. One particular evening after we had stopped to eat, she began to tell me some of her background.

"I believe in God," Toni said, her voice loud enough others in the restaurant could hear, "I just believe if you ask, you're going to receive. To my way of thinking, my parents, my momma always used to say, 'Put it in God's hands. When you get real tired of it, put it in God's hands. There has to be a reason for it.'

"So, when my car broke down, I said, 'God! What is the purpose for all this. You brought us here, like you took all those people in the desert and they said, Why'd you bring us into the desert? Just to die!'

"I got mad. I was talking to God like I'm talking to you. I said, 'Listen God. I'm tired of this. You brought us over here. If you didn't want us over here, why didn't you leave us over there. Closer to home. Why'd the car break down way over here?'

"I said, 'You can have it. I don't want it. There has to be a reason. Why don't you show me why.'

"Then you showed up. It is kind of strange. You don't know the people that end up helping you. The first thing a lot of people tell you is not to talk to strangers. That's kind of hard for me to do. I haven't learned that lesson, yet.

"My momma's Cherokee. My daddy's Mexican-Indian. My grandparents didn't want my momma to marry my daddy because, see, my momma's…is really white complexion. They didn't like him. They wanted her to marry an Indian.

"My daddy said that he liked my momma but there was no way he could get to her, so he used to talk to her grand-grandmomma. That's how they met—by my grand-grandmomma who wanted my daddy to marry my momma because she felt he was a good man. My daddy was twenty-five when they got married and my momma was seventeen. My mother was from Cherokee and when she got married they went to Texas.

"They had twenty kids. She said she didn't know how it happened. It's kind of hilarious. That was during the time they didn't have color television. Why would you have so many kids? I can barely take care of three. My mother was forty-two when she had my baby brother.

"I used to think that the doctor would come into the house and he would bring the baby in his doctor's bag. See, when my brother was born we were living in this house. The doctor came with a black bag. My momma's pretty, my momma's real pretty but when your momma is always fat, you don't know when she's pregnant, not if your parents don't explain anything about sex to you. How do you expect . . . I mean . . . if my parents didn't tell me all about this how was I supposed to know?

"Anyway this guy came with a bag, a black bag. My momma said he was coming to visit. I'm playing out there in the yard and he comes out and he looks at me, and he says, 'You know what? You just had a little brother.'

"I said, 'I did! Where did you have it? In that black bag?'

"He goes, 'Yeah.'

"'Seriously?'

"'It's true.'"

"I believe in curanderos, 'cause one time my momma was sick. Somebody had put a spell on my momma. This lady didn't like my momma and she told her she was going to die. She was jealous, because my daddy treated my momma really nice.

"My daddy loves my momma and they were jealous of my momma, so they put some kind of spell on her. They wanted to get rid of her. So they gave my momma the drink so she would die.

"She used to run the streets with no clothes at night. But the one thing she never left was the Bible."

"Something would come over her, the curandera, like another spirit. She would tell you things you did during the day."

"There was this lady and my momma went over to see her and she offered her something to drink because it was hot. So, my momma just drank it. She doesn't trust people, but she knew this lady. So she drank it and she got real sick. She was pregnant. Instead of my momma dying, the baby died.

"My daddy says my momma got real sick, cause my momma started losing her mind. Sometimes she would be talking to us and she would not remember who we were. She would think she was somebody else. One time she was talking to me and she told me she was that lady.

"And I got mad at her, and I said, 'No, you're not.' I said, 'You're my momma and you better leave that body.'

"I hugged her and five minutes later my momma collapsed. Then she said, 'What happened to me?'

"So I told her. I said, 'You were arguing with me. You told me that you didn't love me, you didn't care about me. But you wasn't my momma. You had somebody else—somebody else's voice.'

"She was evil.

"They did that because they wanted to see my daddy get tired of her and not pay the bills for her, the hospital bills and everything.

"She used to run the streets with no clothes at night. But the one thing she never left was the Bible. She used to always run around with her Bible in her hand, no clothes. She just left the house and she left us there, me and my sisters and brothers. I was only about seven or eight years old then. She left us there. She didn't care about us. It was scary, because I was taking care of my baby brothers.

"Then, one time she said she was real, real sick and this lady that we knew used to come visit us and she told us, 'You know, your momma is going to die.'

"We started crying, because we were real little. We went, 'We don't want our momma to die.'

"She says, 'Let's pray.'

"So we started crying really hard. All my brothers and sisters, we were lying in the bed where my momma was.

"My momma said that she felt that she left her body. She felt she was going up and there was some doves and the doves just closed the door and sent her back.

"She said she told God that she didn't want to die until my baby brother was raised and gone. Right now, my baby brother is still living in the same house that she is.

"She went to the curandera, because my grandparents, my grandmomma was still living. And my grandmomma told her about this lady and that they were going to take her there and the curandera was going to take care of her.

"So she went to stay in Mexico, where the curanderos are. They kept her there. Then, she finally came to her senses and she sent for us to go over there and live with her, 'cause my daddy was working in Florida.

"They sent a telegram to my daddy to tell him that my momma was going to die, that she was real sick, that she was going to die. My daddy had a truck and the truck would only go twenty-five miles an hour and that's from Florida to Texas.

"My daddy said when he got to Mexico where my momma was, there was a funeral going through and he thought that my momma had died. But the thing is that the person that gave her the drink had died and it was her funeral."

"We used to go visit this place where my momma was—the curandera's home. There was a lot of people there. A lot of people used to come there and they used to sing a lot. Sometimes we used to stay until one or two o'clock in the morning.

"The way she used to do things—she used to mix up mud or something and if you had a pain, she would put it where you were hurting and she would use her hands and you wouldn't feel the pain any more, whatever was bothering you. But she used to tell us, 'You can't take it off until the next morning. You can't wash it.'

"If you had the mud stuff on your face, you couldn't wash it, you can't take it off. So sometimes she did this to my brothers and sisters. She never did it to me, because I was the odd person.

"Something would come over her, the curandera, like another spirit. She would tell you things you did during the day. How did this person know about you?

"This person, she could get this spirit anywhere she was. Like sometimes she would be walking around with another person and this person would try to make her angry or something and she would be like somebody else and she could lift up a car if she had to. Pretty powerful lady.

"I used to try to figure it out, how it went. They said you had to sing. I didn't know how to sing.

"They used to sing one song that was called Nino Pedancio. Nino Pedancio was a guy that . . . he was a guy, spirit, that used to come into her, to that lady. Pedancio was his name, but they used to call him 'child.' Child Pedancio.

"When we sang that song, Pedancio would come back through her. While he was there, we couldn't go to sleep. Sometimes we were up to two and three o'clock in the morning, still sitting there and waiting for him to leave. Sometimes he didn't want to go. He would say, 'I don't want to go. I hate to leave you people, you so nice.'

"I would say, 'Would you please go so I can go to sleep.'

"His voice was in her, but it was different than her voice.

"The song brought him there. They had to sing for him to come down. Once you got in there, nobody could leave. Nobody could come in after it started, and nobody could leave. Everybody had to stay there until he was gone, 'cause they said, 'If you leave, that will be bad. Something will happen.'

"I believe in it, since my momma is okay, I do. I do have belief that it was good.

"Still, a lot of people just think it's coincidence. I don't think it's coincidence. I think it was meant to be. You can fight it all you want, but if it's meant to be, it's going to happen.

"This really happened in my family. It's not like I made up a story, because I was there.

"Now I tell my children that if you believe and you ask, it will happen. Sometimes it may take time for it to happen, but it's going to happen. To me, it's just natural."

By the time we headed southwest across New Mexico, leaving Toni to Interstate 40, a bond had developed. We found it hard to let them go it alone, especially with the tears streaming down Michelle's bronze face. But, it was time. Not once while we traveled together had our temperature warning light come back on, and never had we stopped to even inquire as to what our problem might have been to cause us to turn into the rest area where we encountered Toni and her daughters.

After going our separate ways, literally pulling Chris and Michelle apart, the three of us drove from Amarillo diagonally across New Mexico to the Arizona border before stopping for the night. The next day we decided that we would head for Mexicali. Our plans changed, however, when the radiator blew. After taking a half a day in Tucson for repairs, exhaustion forced us to get a room in Yuma.

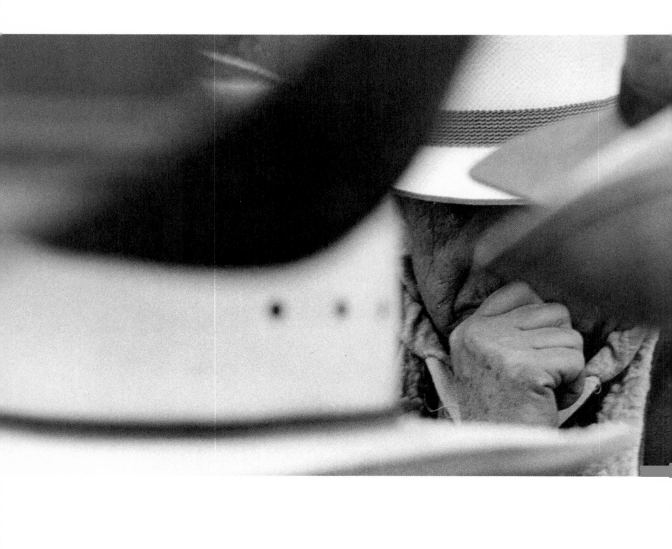

19

MEETING THE TEACHER

Leandis showed up at the motel in Yuma at three o'clock in the morning. With the insistent rapping on the door, James jumped straight up out of bed trying to wake up and figure out what the commotion was. Startled, I raised up with my eyes barely able to open. Focusing them was out of the question, but I could faintly see James's form go for the door.

When I was coherent enough, I asked James what he was doing and flopped back down on the pillow. In the meantime, Chris tried to pull himself out of a deep sleep. He couldn't. His head moved a little, then he turned over and was out for the rest of the night.

The next thing I knew, Leandis was in front of me. I heard myself groggily asking, "How did you get here? How did you know where to find us?" as I wearily roused myself from the bed.

Leandis sidestepped the question with only, "I've kept up with you, kept up with the three of you, all of the way out here."

Then, he landed a shocking blow. Taking a chair, he proclaimed, "Your trip is over. You can go home now. There's no need for you to go on with me to Baja. You have met my teacher."

I was only half dressed, but I was fully awake.

"You came close to an understanding of your trip when you stated to James that you knew you were on a journey to be aware of the happenings along the way, but somehow that went right through your head and out. You spent more time worrying about car trouble or about having kidney stones again. You even told your wife, 'It's all an experience.' Close."

I looked over at James. His expression said it all, as he sat listening and smoking one cigarette after another. He was dumbfounded.

Leandis didn't let up. He had driven with relatives all the way from the Texas border town of Boquillas without stopping, except for gasoline and a snack or two. Now, he had something important to say.

Just Have Faith

All you have to do is just have faith. You've been out there messing around and forgot about the whole thing. All that I've tried to tell you, it's fine as long as it's just ideas. When it gets to be reality, you think things come apart. This is what I want you to realize. Look back at what happened. Just look back and tell me how all of this could have come about if everything was just coincidence, or if something was guiding and directing you.

You forgot what you were doing and why you were doing it. You thought you would get out here and it would happen, but it's been happening ever since you left. You came for the experience. You came to live some truths.

You were so concerned with your little problems, you didn't realize what was going on. Instead of knowing that you were here in the midst of the POWER working, you were being taught to have faith like when you were a child and taught that there was a power that would take care of you.

You were told that you're working for the Creator, working for the One, working for the good. In other words, you were working for the God within you and the God you're within. Somehow you forgot that.

You've had a lot of teachers in a lot of places and a lot of lessons in a lot of places, and you've had the influence of some very high spiritual and intelligent people. The problem is that truth has always been here, but it's so fragmented with a little bit of this and a little bit of that and so distorted in concepts and ideas, until you're starving to death or dying of thirst and there's water all around you.

You scream, "I need," and the supply's already here. But if you don't know what the fruit looks like, you could starve to death in a garden.

I left you on your own for a while. I wanted to see if you could handle my not being there to call on. In the spirit I've been there all the time.

You had to come to realize that there's no good and bad, none of this was good and none of this was bad. You judged it as you went along and made it good or bad.

What you did with each situation, you decided if something was good or, if it was painful, you judged it to be bad. But without what you called bad, other things would not have happened.

Good and bad are human things. There isn't any good or bad in the animal kingdom. There isn't any good or bad. What you call bad isn't necessarily bad. Your life has been like your trip. Without the breakdowns in your life, you wouldn't have the whole picture. There's a purpose in everything. Don't go out and hang yourself because of a lesson.

What about the first person who stopped to help you? You didn't realize that was a good person. A man that took his time. It wasn't part of his job to help with the car. He did this out of the goodness of his heart.

What about the second, third, fourth time you broke down? Every time there was a person who stopped and helped. You may have had to wait a while, but someone stopped to help. You would never have met any of those people if you had not broken down.

And what about meeting that woman and her three daughters at a rest stop outside of Ozark? Do you think that was a coincidence?

You almost killed yourself over something that was a lesson to teach you something. It was just a lesson to get your attention, because you can so easily get off the path. Your experiences are just allusions to a deeper truth in the bigger plan, but you think them to be so real at the time that you get too caught up in them and lose yourself in the process.

Experiences are only what you judge them to be at the time, but they are not reality. You have to get beyond the illusion of what you think them to be and see what they really are. They are merely lessons you asked for at some time. Go below the surface, go deeper. Remember, you get what you ask for. Don't let your lessons destroy you or you'll miss the

"In this term of shadows, what greater shadow could there be for human beings than greed, fear, hatred, and total disregard for human brothers?"

point and you'll miss out on what the Creator has prepared for you.

You've been going out to talk to others, to get information, but you've got to realize that it's in you. It's not in somebody else. You can get wisdom from the same place they get it. The true teacher always comes from within.

There are no special gifts, there are only abilities that fit into the puzzle. It comes from the spirit, within and without, and man has to discover his relationship with that spirit. You must recognize God in everyone and everything.

Look at your life. Had your life been different, you wouldn't be here now. It's not where you're going, it's the trip itself.

Shadows

This was a "show me" trip. It was meant to show you there are balances. You saw apathy and you saw the compassion some have for others. On the surface it looked to you like there were no more honest, caring people. But you found that there are some left.

You're working with elders on understanding what you're here for, what you're doing, who you are, and what life's about. Yet, you get out here and you look around. It looks like your world has fallen apart. People will cut your throat for enough money to buy one drug hit. There seems to be no regard for anything except individual selfishness. So you got a little cynical. You don't even stop, you don't help people, because you feel that you're being endangered.

In this term of shadows, what greater shadow could there be for human beings than greed, fear, hatred, and total disregard for human brothers?

What is the shadow?

Shadows are the dark side of reality. If you live in the shadows, if you rush from one shadow to another shadow, then you're avoiding the light.

When you avoid the light, you're avoiding exposure, or being seen, or being noticed, or taking a stand.

The Two Paths

You're going one of two ways. You're either on the spiritual path or on the material path. If you're on a material path, go ahead and think you're the best or try to be the best. Get it however you can. That's what that's about.

If you're going to get yourself on the spiritual path, then you're going to have to decide. You're either going to have to work for yourself or work for the Creator. You're going to work for the One or yourself. If you're looking for praise and fame, you've got a problem because you're seeking the praise. If you don't get it, then you're setting yourself up for a big fall. If you're seeking the praise and anybody has anything to say negative about you, then you've got to take the blame. If you're working for yourself, then you've got to accept both praise and blame.

But if you're seeking neither praise nor blame, you're just doing the work for the Creator, doing the work for the good of life, then it doesn't matter. You're not working for others. If you're trying to become a part of a higher expression, don't worry about praise. Don't worry about blame. They'll both trap you. They'll both grind your ass in the ground. They'll both teach you a lesson, because they're the wrong gods to worship. If you think I'm joking you, try it!

The Way of the Spirit

I can give you my experience, and that's a story. I experienced it. You only heard it. But when you go and experience something, then you are telling a story. The difference is, if you're repeating a story, there's no spirit in it. When you experience it, there's spirit in it. So you put spirit in the story. This is your story.

There used to be a ritual among the spiritual people. I call them the spiritual people because they were the original people and in touch with their own spirit and the spirit of everything else. By the time a child, a male child, reached a certain age, he would have been taught to hunt, he would have been taught the skills to connect with the spirit. When the elders judged it to be the right time, he was taken out in the middle of the desert and left. He was given three days to return home. He was left in an area he was not familiar with, so he had to follow the spirit to find food, the spirit to find water. That was just to seek his vision quest.

Up until that point he had been told of the power of the spirit, now it was up to him to experience it. You may say this was cruel, but actually he wasn't left alone. Someone knew where he was all the time, but they couldn't interfere unless it was a matter of life and death—not what he thought was life and death, but life and death in the judgment of these who were watching after him. Unless he returned back fulfilled and in touch with the spirit enough to get home, then he did not become a man. That would have been an embarrassment. Actually, he would rather die in the desert than be rescued.

"I was taught that God was love, God loved everybody, God loved the little children and that God protected and took care of the little children."

This wasn't cruelty. This was a matter of necessity. He had to survive by understanding the way the spirit had created and how it expressed. He had to understand he had to develop or break through his intuition.

People today don't understand the spirit at all. To the white person, a spirit is generally thought of as something evil. In reality the church has lost all touch with the spiritual. What it has become is a ritual and a set of rules.

It works like this. Each religion has a box with a lot of symbols on it, but the box is sealed. It has a nice ribbon around it, and what they say is, "The spirit is in the box. The truth is in the box, but to open the box is blasphemy. If you open the box, God is going to punish you. You don't look inside the box. Forget this spirit business. Just do what we tell you. Come to church on Sunday, bring your money, leave your money, and go home. Come back next Sunday. Bring someone with you. Tell him to bring his money, leave it in the box and go home, but don't open the box. You can bring it every Sunday, but don't open it."

Suppose you go to the library, you want to know what's in this box. You start looking, questioning, and start studying. You start understanding, and you're opening the box with each understanding. When you finally look in the box, there's nothing in the box. The box is empty. You find that the box is just an object.

The box is the same thing as the medicine man carrying feathers. The only problem with that is that there's an understanding of the spirit with the medicine man. There's a spiritual understanding, whether he's got roots or herbs. Those are mediums, mediums that are necessary because the people need something to believe in. An example would be the power of a pill in healing for the white man.

Spiritual Healing

For many years healers, curanderos or medicine men, have been seen as being evil, mysterious. Why do people have the idea that a curandero is a sorcerer, that he is a sort of a witch doctor, and that all that he does is evil? People don't understand that there have always been spiritual healers, because their work was labeled as being the work of the devil. But this type of healing was in place here on this land, the Americas, before the white man, before the Spanish, the English, or the French, in general, all the people who ever came and brought Christianity. If they tell you it's in this church or that set of rules, don't believe them. They don't know what they're talking about.

I can remember being a little guy, about six years old. The church came in and told us our ways were wrong. The priests then taught their religion. The idea I was taught was that God was love, God loved everybody, God loved the little children and that God protected and took care of the little children. Also that God was there with you all the time. You even had a guardian angel. It was a beautiful wonderful thing. It made you love God or want to love God like you loved your mother and your father.

Suddenly when you're about eight or ten years old, they tell you this isn't so. Now, you've got to go repent because you sinned and you're going to hell. Well, the day before I hadn't done anything. Now I'm going to hell. This worried me. It worried me for a long time.

They had me so convinced I wasn't sure that I had made the grade. It still worried me.

Then they started saying that there was a Second Coming and that all these dead people were going to rise up, all going to come up out of the ground. There's going to be hands flying here and over there and everything. There's going to be two people working in the field. One's going to be taken and the other's going to be left. This bothered me.

This was going to be so bad. I just didn't think this God that I once was told about...he'd gotten so far away. He was with me ever since I was a little child, now they've taken him so far away that I was afraid that he had forgotten about me. There was no way I could get in touch with him. I was scared to death about this.

It was July and it was hot. I had an idea about what hell was like because I was working in the field. My momma and I were working in the field. I figured that if there was anyone ever good enough to go to heaven it would have been my momma.

We were out there working and I got to thinking about this thing. I got to thinking it was about time He would come any minute and I knew with me and my momma out there together—well, as good as my momma was, I would be the one left.

I just literally got so carried away with this thing, I just lost it. Passed out right there in the middle of the field. What made me pass out was a thunderstorm that came up and lightning hit close to us and this big line of thunder rolled and I thought He had come. Down I went. Scared my mother nearly to death.

She got over to me and began slapping me in the face. She didn't know if I had been hit by lightning or what so she carried me to the house. She carried me to the house and put me to bed. The only good thing about that was that I was sick and didn't have to go to that church.

Before Christianity

Before the white man came with his religion, this land was a spiritual place. The people who lived here, particularly in the barren areas where food and water was scarce, realized that everything—beginning with the earth—had a spirit. Everything had an individual expression, a real expression, because there was a different spirit in every living thing.

They knew that everything that existed was an individual expression of the Creator. They understood the fact that there was one Great Spirit and that Great Spirit was divided in the same manner as animals are divided into male and female. Plants are divided into male and female. Humans are divided into male and female. So they called the earth female and the sun male. This did not mean they worshipped the sun or the earth. They worshipped the Creator, they worshipped these expressions of the Creator in the sense that they gave thanks to the Mother Earth. They gave thanks for the sun, for the moon, for all things. They gave thanks for the first plants that brought new food and new life in the spring. They gave thanks for everything that was provided for them.

They gave thanks for water. When they did a rain dance, they were not doing a pagan dance. They were doing a dance of thanksgiving for the blessing they were about to receive.

To give thanks for something you are about to receive is called faith. It works, because there are laws involved. Some understood, some didn't, but it worked and it still works. Everything had its own spirit, its own existence, not only in the physical, but in the spiritual or in the higher form. So they were very much in tune with the same Creator you call God.

If one of my ancestors was out someplace and needed food or needed water, he didn't get excited and say, "I'm going to die of thirst," and just sit down under the first bush he came to. He gave thanks to the Creator, and he knew the Creator would provide it for him.

It could be said he followed his intuition, others may say instinct, but instinct is something that comes from the animal, something that's built in. Intuition is when you decide something, it's when you power it into being. You know it's going to be there.

So he followed his intuition to water, to food, to an area bearing fruit, or to an area where there were animals. Before taking anything, he gave thanks to the Creator for, first of all, bringing him to it. Then, he gave thanks to the animal and asked permission of the animal for his life to sustain his.

He knew that the order of things was that the higher always had dominion over the lower. Yet, at the same time, he realized that in the spirit

"With every person you come in contact with, you tie one string on to you and to them."

all things were connected and that he was responsible, also, for the protection of that animal. He took nothing that he had no use for. There was no slaughtering of animals by the people of the spirit in that period. He only took what he needed. He didn't destroy the land or the vegetation.

Although he may not have known the laws involved, he knew the action to set the laws into motion. He knew certain things. Thanksgiving was one, intuition was another, and not to let emotions interfere with his actions. He knew enough about these things and was close enough to the spirit until he could exist on any part of this land, regardless of how barren it seems to you today.

The same thing was true of healing. He healed the land, the land healed him. He healed the animal, the animal healed him. He healed the animal in spirit, as well as by giving thanks.

This made him a higher spiritual individual. Then, as today, not all of the people understood the great depths of the spirit. There were a few who understood it more than others. These became the elders, medicine men, the teachers, the spiritual leaders. They were more in touch with their inner spirit and the outer spirit of the things around them.

They could call on the laws of healing. They could draw the power of their inner being and give blessing to certain objects, to certain herbs, certain potions, that would give them an effect on illness. They had chants and prayers that affected the person who was ill, because they set up a bond with this same force that created them. They knew very well that any force that has the power, the knowledge, the wisdom, to create something has the equal power, knowledge, and wisdom to heal.

The Law of Cause and Effect

Medicine men knew that everything is the effect of a cause and everything is the cause of an effect. If you take a life, you may have to make a choice over here concerning a life. The effects relate to the cause of the action, but the circumstance may be so far apart that there's no way to look at it and figure out where it came from. In this life, you create some-thing here, and you meet something down the way somewhere.

This over here may have affected one person in one way because of some quirk he's got, but this over here may affect you totally differently by a different quirk, but the cause and effect are equal.

In everything, it's the same time under the law of cause and effect. This thing is operating equally. The law is coming out perfectly every time. The problem is we don't always know the law, and the second problem is we are personally involved in the circumstances, so we don't see the whole picture. We see it from our point of view. The trouble with our point of view is the guy you're talking about at the other end of the effect has a totally different point of view. Everything he's doing, every-thing he's not doing is for a different reason. It's a big pot of stew.

What we need to do is to know the law—the laws of the body, the laws of the mind, and the laws of the soul. Everything is part of the uni-versal law. What we have to do is work in harmony with that law regardless of what the circumstances are. If we do that, then everything equalizes out. But, what we tend to do is work with our idea of what is in harmony from our own selfish viewpoint. So that doesn't mean it's necessarily in harmony with the law. See!

So what we're doing is stirring the stew more. So that means that the effect is meeting us down the road in a different pattern. Until we use reason to the point of perfection, then we don't become intuitive. When we use what we've got and perfect that, then it automatically becomes intuition. If you've got perfect reason, you're automatically intuitive. That's the next step.

Reason is to the human what instinct is to the animal and what intu-ition is to God. Those are the things consciousness revolves around. They're the center of the storm.

Right now we're in a muddled mess. We don't know what the cause was and now we're trying to deal with the effect that directly affected us.

Who knows why that boy stopped to help you with your car? The whole cause could have been to give him an opportunity for an effect that he needed, but who knows that. You didn't know and still don't. You only saw that breakdown from your viewpoint. But what about all the people that passed you by. What was their cause and effect?

Once you take a responsibility, see it through. You have taken it on, because it has become cause and effect to you—not only to you but everybody else.

The problem with cause and effect is the fact that it's like a bunch of strings. With every person you come in contact with, you tie one string on to you and to them. You either have to satisfy this and release that connection on mutual agreement or then you're tied to that person or that thing through cause and effect from now on until it's satisfied.

If there is anything that directly causes pain or problems, particularly if it's deliberate, then you must go and work it out directly with that person.

The main thing is not what happened, it's the action you're taking minute by minute and not the action you took yesterday. You look back and say I got this done and I got that done, I had this problem and that one—that's not what mattered. It was moment by moment because you live in the eternal now. There is no time. Time is an illusion.

You got more information on the trip when you sat around and talked among yourselves and when you got out and talked to people than if you had made it to Baja. Like that kid that came along in Memphis. There was a guy that made no bones about anything. Remember when he was asked why he stopped. He said, "My daddy used to do this. He stopped and helped people. And I've always done it, too."

That was just as beautiful, as good, and had all the same meanings of the Creative power as the so-called story of the Good Samaritan had in the Bible. There wasn't any difference in it. Everyone tends to think, "Oh, that's a beautiful story, there's just not people like that anymore."

There are people like that.

The story of Creation, that's a story. This is Creation. Creation isn't something that happened, Creation is something that is. It is.

The Story of the Gods

There's a story that the gods were talking one day, all gathered up, and they said, "Wait a minute now. Here we got man and he's got all this power. He's got all this potential. Man is a part of us. Man is God, but he

"You came out here looking for the answers, really for your power. You thought someone was going to hand it to you or tell you more stories. I've told you all I can. It was within you all the time."

hasn't come to the point to where he knows what to do with this. What are we going to do?"

They said, "We've got to hide it from him."

One said, "Let's put it in the bottom of the ocean."

Another said, "No, no, he'll go down there. Eventually he'll go down there. He'll find it."

"Let's put it up in the sky."

"No, no, one day he's going to fly up there. He'll be up there. He'll find it."

"Well, let's bury it deep in the earth."

"No. He'll dig. He'll dig it up."

"Well, where are we going to put it?"

One said, "Let's go to the big god, the wisest of all, and ask him."

So they went to the wisest and they asked, "Where are we going to hide this from man?"

He said, "Put it within him. He'll never look there."

The agile curandero's stories were over. Now, his eyes bore intensely into mine. Then, he said, "You came out here looking for the answers, really for your power. You thought someone was going to hand it to you or tell you more stories. I've told you all I can. It was within you all the time.

"Do you remember asking me after the healing session how I did those things? I said, 'Come with me. I want you to meet my teacher.'

"You wanted to know where my teacher was and I said, 'Come with me.' Well, you came. Now, your trip is over. You can go home. You have met my teacher."

MEETING THE TEACHER

• • •

Leandis was ready to go. Opening the door and standing half in and half out, with the blazing light of the morning sun flooding the dim room, he became impatient. The oppressive desert heat rushed in, replacing the chill of the air conditioning. He waited, but it was obvious he would not wait long.

"Tell me this," I asked him. "It has been on my mind ever since the healing ceremony. What did you whisper to that woman when you leaned over her? Was it private?"

"Ho," he shot back. "I told her, like I've tried to tell you, she was a spiritual being. That she was perfect, she was a reflection of the Creator. And, when the physical reflects the spirit, there is perfection. Healing must take place."

"Will she get the message?" I asked.

"She may, but probably not. Most want someone to save them, to save them from themselves and their unbelief."

Putting his weight on one leg and resting the other, he went on, hurrying to be on his way. "You! What will I do with you? You have thought the experiences real and you thought the shadows of those experiences that were following you were demons. You made that up. Because you are like the Creator in that you can create, you made up your own demons.

"That wasn't you. You are spirit. Only the spirit is real. The physical is the shadow. The shadow is a reflection of the soul or spirit. Your experiences are only echoes of where the physical has been or is going. It's hard to figure out if the echo is past or future, because the echo is only a bouncing back. Shadows and echoes are not real. Only the spirit is real. The problem is that it's as hard to see as it is to define. But! It's real, more real than anything you'll ever encounter in this life.

"Go on, discover your truth. It's up to you, and you alone, because no one can do it for you. It's yours and no one else's. You're on your own.'"

As he turned to go, I spurted out, half-demanding, "How did you find us? How did you know we would be here? This motel? I thought we were supposed to meet you in three or four days. It's been seven. How? Why?" I asked, wanting to pull him back in and get my questions answered. As far as I knew, I would never see him again and I wanted everything answered before he left.

When he looked as if he was about to speak, I blurted out one more question. "Why would you do all this for me?" I asked.

He chuckled, "Everything's an exchange. Why did you choose me?"

Then, he backtracked and answered my previous barrage of questions with his own. "Why did it take you seven days? Why did you choose this motel? Why did you stop in Yuma? And, why had you lost hope of finding me?"

I started to respond, but he stopped me by saying, "I have people waiting. There are sick to attend to." And the door closed with a click behind him.

I looked at James, then over to Chris, who was curled up into a ball and still asleep, and back to James. For a long time we just looked at each other. Finally, James was the first to speak. "I came out here as a favor to you and to have a little vacation. I wanted to meet old Leandis, you'd talked so much about him. Now I've met him. I think I've learned more in a few hours than I have listening to all those Ivy League guys in pinstriped suits. One thing's for sure. That old man's a real character. I've heard about people like him, but I swear to you, I never figured on meeting one. Nobody does what he's done. Nobody."

Then he hesitated, scratching his head.

"What is it?" I quizzed and waited for him to respond.

"I know we're going home, but there's one thing I'd like to ask and then I'm going back to bed."

Nodding that whatever he wanted I was willing to agree to, I muttered, "Just say it. Go on, give it to me."

"Nothing like that," he laughed, not worrying about waking Chris. "It's just that I've never been to California. I told a lot of people I was going, and I'd just like to cross the border to say I got there. You know, in a little town like Toccoa word gets around. A lot of people'll be asking about my trip."

He and I got so tickled we both nearly fell into the floor. "Yeah, yeah, we can do that. No problem. You got it."

I sat on the side of my bed while he crawled into his. "Going to bed, aren't you?" he asked, pulling the sheets up to his chin.

"In a minute. I think I'll sit here and sort out some things first. I'll sleep better," I said.

Soon his breathing grew deeper, intermingling with short snorts. Then, falling into the warm envelope of a welcomed sleep, his snoring revved up. Needing to find my own private space for quiet and solitude, I eased up off the bed, walked ever so lightly across the room, and went into the bathroom. Closing the door, I turned on the light. The old fluorescent light buzzed and

MEETING THE TEACHER

flickered, then finally popped on. Motionless, I stood in front of the mirror in the dim blue-green light just looking into my own eyes for a long time.

I had always practiced in my photography the old philosophy that the eyes were the gateway to the depths of the soul. In my work with people I had concentrated on the eyes, because I felt that they revealed the life of the individual. Maybe to some degree the superstition of some indigenous groups had a basic element of truth to it when they refused to have their photographs made because they believed the camera could capture their souls. I had never bought into the idea, but I believed that the photograph could contain a reflection of the soul, especially if the picture showed the eyes. Now, as I gazed into the reflection of my own eyes, I was ready to see if I could somehow make contact with my soul.

It was a strange experience peering eye to eye with myself. For decades I had stood before mirrors to carry out the rituals of hygiene and grooming or to look for some nonexistent illness, as I had done in my depression, but never had I practiced the feat I was now undertaking. At first, I felt awkward, embarrassed at my foolishness. Nevertheless, as I held the stare, it was as if I was seeing someone else. I could not say that I saw my soul or even a reflection of it, but there was something I connected with. Needing to push myself further, I said very quietly to the image in front of me, "I'm healthy. I'm not in any imminent danger of dying. Someday, yes, but not right at this moment. I'm going to live."

Then, surprising myself, I added, "And, I'm not damned either."

Blinking, I stepped back, breaking the hold of the reflection. Damnation, I thought. Where did that come from? Leandis had hinted at the thought when he said, "There's no right and wrong, just what you've done to create the situation you need."

But, I had been damned! I had been living under a curse I had accepted from long ago. I had left the teachings of the church. That had put me under a curse just as surely as if someone had purposely paid a brujo to cast a spell on me.

I began to reflect. I had been brought up as a strict fundamentalist Baptist. Every time the church doors opened my parents would force me to attend. As a teenager it was guilt that whipped me in. The doctrines had been driven into my conscious and subconscious mind with each sermon. They were a part of me and controlled my thinking in everything I did. God was ever present, always watching to see every move I made and writing down all of my infractions. He was keeping score, I had been taught. And He was a God of judgment and of wrath. If I disobeyed, I would have to purge myself and seek His forgiveness. Each time I transgressed, I would have to start all over with Him. I could never find his favor, much less win at the high stakes of eternal bliss. Over and over I stood not at the portals of the Pearly Gate but at the gaping pit of hell.

To entreat the All Powerful, I yielded. I would be His servant by studying for the ministry. Immediately after high school, I set out upon the ultimate path by enrolling in a Baptist school as my first step in reaching His goal for my life—actually the goal of my church and the burly enforcers of the humanly defined moralist rules who ranted from the pulpit. As young as I was, however, I doubted. When I questioned the interpretations, I was told by ministers and instructors that I was never to question the scriptures. Even to question was a sin that would lead me to eternal damnation, because that was to challenge the authority of the Almighty and the inspiration of the holy texts. If I persisted, I was sternly warned, the devil would snatch a willing disciple out of the warm arms of a loving God.

The seeds of guilt had been planted and the fertile ground for my shadows had been plowed. There were only two choices for me. It would have to be either God or the devil. To follow was to be on God's side and have Him on mine; to disagree was to lose God and fall into the hands of the devil.

Then, I committed the unsurpassable offense. I turned my back on the ministry when I found photography and decided to pursue a career in journalism. But I could not escape. The instructions were clear. It was either God or the devil. Over and over, in sermons I had sat through, it had been proclaimed, "If once you put your hands to the plow and look back, you are not fit for the Kingdom of Heaven." And, of course, once I committed to the higher calling of the ministry, I had put my hands to the plow.

By choosing another profession, I had given up the sacred calling; I had looked back, in the view of the Baptists, and yielded to the devil's worldly lure. Hell would be my reward. I would have its fire and brimstone for eternity. My rebellion in fleeing the repressive doctrine of the church had led me straight past the Kingdom and into the army of the forces of evil. I was doomed.

Damned by the church I left, I went to hell—in their mind and in my own subconscious mind. Photography, a form of catching shadows, was what I was doing in hell.

Even going to the Indians had been a transgression, because I dared to consider the *heresy* of their views of the Creator. The more they shared, the more I wanted to hear. How free they were. With them, the individual made the choice of what path he would walk. His decisions were his, for better or worse, and no one else's. He would have to learn his own lessons. In death, there was no hell to face as there was for Christians. The spirit would go back to the Creator. But, there was no damnation.

What beauty! With the Indians there was only one Creator, and He existed in all of His creation. How could He separate himself from His creation by sending part of Himself to hell?

The message was beginning to come through. I was part of the creation, too, and the Creator was in me. I was connected to all living things; they were a part of me. Nothing could be separate, because everything came from the same source. That's what Leandis had meant when he said, "Blame no one and find no fault. If you do, you are finding fault with the Creator. That is impossible, because the Creator cannot find fault or cast blame on Himself or what He's made. Since you're part of it all, that means you, too."

As I stood in front of the mirror, sequestered within the confines of the bathroom, I said aloud to myself, "I'm not afraid to die. I'm not a coward."

It was not the fear of flying that had so terrorized me, it was the fear of frying eternally on the griddle of the devil. Subconsciously I could smell my own evil grease sizzle over the lake of fire forever. That's why I had been afraid all along.

In my aloneness, I was taken by a revelation. In that moment, as if someone blew a soft breath of cool fresh air across my face, I realized I had never really released myself from the destructive ideas in my subconscious.

"My God," I wanted to shout, "that's it. That's why I've done things the way I have, and why I've lived under shadows for so long. I have to release them." Then, with a newfound peace, I took a deep breath and said, "I'm ready."

I never did go back to bed. As soon as James got up, he rushed out the door for coffee. I roused Chris, and he and I dressed, packed, and started loading the car. By midafternoon we were on the road to, yes, California. In four days, without a hint of car trouble, we were back in North Carolina. Within three weeks I was flying again. I was a little nervous, but the fear had lifted.

I had finally caught the ultimate shadow, and it was me.